Cambridge Elements 

Elements in Business Strategy
edited by
J.-C. Spender
Rutgers Business School

HUMANISTIC MANAGEMENT AND LEADERSHIP

Michael Pirson
Fordham University

CAMBRIDGE
UNIVERSITY PRESS

Shaftesbury Road, Cambridge CB2 8EA, United Kingdom

One Liberty Plaza, 20th Floor, New York, NY 10006, USA

477 Williamstown Road, Port Melbourne, VIC 3207, Australia

314–321, 3rd Floor, Plot 3, Splendor Forum, Jasola District Centre,
New Delhi – 110025, India

Cambridge University Press is part of Cambridge University Press & Assessment,
a department of the University of Cambridge.

We share the University's mission to contribute to society through the pursuit of
education, learning and research at the highest international levels of excellence.

www.cambridge.org
Information on this title: www.cambridge.org/9781009698443
DOI: 10.1017/9781009698412

© Michael Pirson 2026

This publication is in copyright. Subject to statutory exception and
to the provisions of relevant collective licensing agreements, no reproduction
of any part may take place without the written permission of
Cambridge University Press & Assessment.

When citing this work, please include a reference to the DOI 10.1017/9781009698412

First published 2026

A catalogue record for this publication is available from the British Library

*A Cataloging-in-Publication data record for this Element is available from
the Library of Congress*

ISBN 978-1-009-69846-7 Hardback
ISBN 978-1-009-69844-3 Paperback
ISSN 2515-0693 (online)
ISSN 2515-0685 (print)

Cambridge University Press & Assessment has no responsibility for the persistence
or accuracy of URLs for external or third-party internet websites referred to in this
publication and does not guarantee that any content on such websites is, or will
remain, accurate or appropriate.

For EU product safety concerns, contact us at Calle de José Abascal, 56, 1°, 28003
Madrid, Spain, or email eugpsr@cambridge.org.

Humanistic Management and Leadership

Elements in Business Strategy

DOI: 10.1017/9781009698412
First published online: May 2026

Michael Pirson
Fordham University

Author for correspondence: Michael Pirson, pirson@fordham.edu

Abstract: This Element introduces the foundational concepts and practical applications of humanistic management and leadership. Centering on the dual imperative to protect human dignity and promote well-being, it offers a scientifically grounded alternative to economistic models of organizing. The book develops an integrative framework spanning six levels of analysis – individual, relational, team, organizational, societal, and ecological – showing how each level can be designed to meet a dignity threshold while enabling thriving for people and planet. Drawing on contemporary research across management, psychology, the humanities, and the natural sciences, it clarifies core principles, managerial practices, and measurable implications for governance, strategy, culture, and learning. Rich real-world cases illustrate how humanistic enterprises and institutions operationalize these principles to create enduring, regenerative value for employees, customers, communities, investors, and the natural environment. The Element concludes with guidance for educators and practitioners seeking to embed humanistic leadership in everyday decision-making across sectors in practice.

Keywords: dignity, flourishing, well-being, management, leadership

© Michael Pirson 2026

ISBNs: 9781009698467 (HB), 9781009698443 (PB), 9781009698412 (OC)
ISSNs: 2515-0693 (online), 2515-0685 (print)

Contents

Introduction: A Better World Is Possible

The world is in trouble, and we all feel it. Societies are ever more polarized, conflict is on the rise, and humanity's very survival is at stake.[1] Very few of these problems are being addressed powerfully or effectively.[2]

Depression, isolation, and suicide are on the rise and collective sleepwalking is endangering progress that has been hard earned.[3] Democracies are under threat, while dictators with old-style solutions are celebrating an historic comeback, with war once again becoming a constant evil. With human civilization under pressure from ever more people on this planet, our earth is showing clear signals that our current way of life is not sustainable.

The way we lead and manage ourselves does not work!

We know it, we sense it, we feel it in our bones, and we become collectively despondent and resigned.[4]

There is a better way![5]

As John F. Kennedy said: "Our problems are manmade – therefore, they can be solved by man. And man can be as big as he wants. No problem of human destiny is beyond human beings. Man's reason and spirit have often solved the seemingly unsolvable – and we believe they can do it again."[6]

All of our current existential problems are human made. We have built our economic and social systems on a blueprint that does not correspond to human reality. We therefore build poorly and have bad roadmaps. We can redesign and rebuild better.

---

[1]　Much of Sections 1 to 4 has been adapted from my prior writing especially my 2017 book *Humanistic management – protecting dignity and promoting well-being*, published by Cambridge University.

[2]　Bradshaw, C. J., Ehrlich, P. R., Beattie, A., Ceballos, G., Crist, E., Diamond, J., Dirzo, R., Ehrlich, A. H., Harte, J., Harte, M. E., Pyke, G. H., Raven, P. H., Ripple, W. J., Saltré, F., Turnbull, C., Wackernagel, M., & Blumstein, D. T. (2021). Underestimating the challenges of avoiding a ghastly future. *Frontiers in Conservation Science*, *1*, 615419. Max Roser (2022). "The world is awful. The world is much better. The world can be much better." Published online at OurWorldinData.org. Retrieved from: https://ourworldindata.org/much-better-awful-can-be-better

[3]　Booth, J. (2023, October 23). Anxiety statistics and Facts. *Forbes Health*. www.forbes.com/health/mind/anxiety-statistics/

[4]　Scharmer, C. O. (2016). *Theory U: Leading from the future as it emerges.* Berrett-Koehler Publishers; Scharmer, O., & Pomeroy, E. (2024). Fourth person: The knowing of the field. *Journal of Awareness-Based Systems Change*, *4*(1), 19–48.

[5]　Contributors to Friends Central. (n.d.). *The one with the metaphorical tunnel.* Friends Central. https://friends.fandom.com/wiki/The_One_With_The_Metaphorical_Tunnel Joey Tribbiani as Kevin in Friends: Season 3, Episode 4. The One with the Metaphorical Tunnel | Friends Central | Fandom

[6]　Eidenmuller, M. E. (n.d.). *American rhetoric: John F. Kennedy – American University Address.* www.americanrhetoric.com/speeches/jfkamericanuniversityaddress.html

Our basic design flaw is that we use an understanding of ourselves as human beings that is inaccurate at best, and suicidal at worst.[7] We see ourselves as pure market actors, greedy to maximize our own utility at the cost of anything else. In technical terms, we use the blueprint of "homo economicus," or economic human, as the roadmap to build businesses, organizations, and society. Therefore, we build organizations that cater to psychopathic individuals, create human suffering at scale (while solving some relevant human issues), and create a system in which people feel unvalued, unheard, and uncared for.[8]

Albert Einstein famously stated: "We can't solve problems by using the same kind of thinking we used when we created them."[9] Still, the practitioners of mainstream business as well as business school educators struggle to deploy an alternative way of thinking. As William Allen, the former chancellor of the Delaware Court of Chancery, notes, "[o]ne of the marks of a truly dominant intellectual paradigm is the difficulty people have in even imagining an alternative view."[10]

While there is an increasing realization that we must shift, it is unclear whether the current solutions on offer are workable.[11] In this Element, I present a perspective that is grounded in reality, supported by science, aligned with the traditions of ancient wisdom, and that has proven to work better for people, the planet, and also prosperity. With many of my colleagues, I have worked on conceptualizing this much-needed alternative paradigm for business; a humanistic paradigm, one based on the protection of dignity and the promotion of well-being rather than mere wealth. This Element starts by laying out the dominant narrative of the current paradigm; an economistic paradigm focused on acquisition of power, wealth, and status. The basic argument is that our understanding of "who we are as people" fundamentally influences the way we organize individually, in groups, in organizations, and in society. Shifting our understanding of who we are is therefore central to any workable approach.

In the following pages, I will present both narratives on human nature in business: The dominant model represented by "homo economicus," that accurately represents about 1 percent of the population (Section 2),

---

[7] Bregman, R. (2020). *Humankind: A hopeful history*. Bloomsbury Publishing.

[8] Wexler, M. N. (2008). Conjectures on systemic psychopathy: Reframing the contemporary corporation. *Society and Business Review*, *3*(3), 224–238. https://doi.org/10.1108/17465680810907305

[9] Albert Einstein – We can't solve problems by using the… (brainyquote.com)

[10] Allen, W. T. (1993). Contracts and communities in corporation law. *Washington and Lee Law Review*, *50*, 1395–1407.

[11] Fascism, communism, and many forms of tribalism have had harsh consequences in the past.

and the alternative model of "homo sapiens," which better represents the remaining 99 percent of the population (Section 3). While there is scientific evidence to support the latter perspective, the disciplines of economics and management have memetically adopted an understanding based on axiomatic assumptions. The homo economicus worldview of the human being as uncaring and narrowly self-interested has influenced the way business structures are set up (limited liability, focus on profit maximization).[12]

On the other hand, the homo sapiens perspective allows us to understand the importance of care, the notion of human dignity, and the evolutionary reasons why humans only survived when organizing for the common good. In Sections 4 and 5, I will present the basic evidence for the humanistic perspective on management that leads to balancing our innate four drives to acquire, bond, comprehend, and defend. Expressed very succinctly, the argument is that if we attempt to maximize any one of the four drives, we will create conflict and conditions that undermine our survival and thriving. But when we envision organizations as places that balance the four innate drives, we can create spaces in which humanity can flourish. By adopting this perspective, we can envision organizations as caring communities that converge to produce for the benefit of the common good.

In collaboration with the Humanistic Management Association, scholars have chronicled numerous organizations that follow the humanistic paradigm, which focuses on the protection of human dignity and the promotion of societal well-being and flourishing. Some of these organizations will be highlighted in Section 6. The fact that many such organizations are run successfully and oftentimes more profitably over time proves that alternatives to the current economistic or tribalistic understanding of organizing exist.

I close with the argument presented by humanistic management scholars suggesting that a focus on human dignity, understood as that which escapes all price mechanisms (Kant) and is valued intrinsically (freedom, love, care, responsibility, character, and ethics) can challenge the theoretical accuracy of current paradigms. In addition, if the end goal of organizing were expanded to include well-being or common good, scholars can better understand how business plays an active role in solving current global problems. As a result, practitioners, managers, and leaders can adopt this humanistic mindset for their own benefit and that of those they are privileged to lead.

---

[12] Easterbrook, F. H., & Fischel, D. R. (1996). *The economic structure of corporate law.* Harvard University Press.

1 The Need for a New Paradigm in Management

A Failing Narrative

Meet Elisabeth, my neighbor. Elisabeth did all she was told to succeed in life.[13] After earning an MBA at a reputable school, she chose to work for a hospital. She wanted to stay true to her desire to serve others and thought the healthcare industry would allow her to do so. One afternoon, we run into each other as she is walking her dog. I ask her how she likes her work and she confesses, "Oh my god, it is so stressful…I never really wanted to be in this competitive, businessy type of environment but it seems the hospital is just as corporate and mean-spirited as anything else…"

Meet John, formerly a successful Wall Street banker. He joined the world of banking because he admired its service orientation, but quit the industry in what he later described as a midlife crisis. The more he thought about the type of work his bank was doing and the people with whom it was working, the more depressed he had become. He had an especially hard time reconciling what he heard in church on Sunday with the values of the financial industry. The culture of banking and service that he admired had turned into something he could not be a part of. So he decided to get out.

Meet Natalia, a popular bartender, who tells me she is about to quit her job because of the toxic work culture. Competition for tips has become cutthroat, the waiting staff are highly mistrusting, and the apparent favorites among the owners are those that bring in the money yet hurt their peers by cheating them out of their wages, tips, and clients. Drinks recipes get remastered to be cheaper, quality is becoming less important, and no honorable waiter wants to serve "shitty drinks." As a result, the atmosphere at the bar becomes hostile and customers that came for the homey atmosphere now go elsewhere. As the downward spiral continues, more "good people" quit, the bar has to invest more in advertising and marketing to capture new clients, which increases their costs and requires new cost-cutting efforts elsewhere, such as hiring wait staff for 5.25 USD/hour on emergency terms, all of which creates high levels of turnaround. As a result, the atmosphere is becoming ever more transactional and the bar can only compete on price, which attracts ever fickler clientele. When Natalia shares her observations, the owners justify their decisions with "that is how business is done around here."

---

[13] Much of Sections 1 to 4 has been adapted from my prior writing, especially my 2017 book, "Humanistic Management: Protecting Dignity and Promoting Well-Being," published by Cambridge University.

Elisabeth, John, and Natalia are not poor and have the luxury of many choices. In many ways, they are privileged. These real-life stories highlight a shared unhappiness that exists despite privilege. While one could easily wave aside such unhappiness as a minority view, research shows that, despite unprecedented levels of material wealth, people are increasingly alienated at work and are looking to redefine the meaning of success. On the flipside, an increasing number of people wish to engage in more meaningful activities at work and beyond, and sense an urgency to be part of the solution to the many problems humanity is facing (climate change, terrorism, social inequality, and poverty).[14]

Mainstream thinking about the business world has become associated with the fictional character of Gordon Gekko and his motto: "Greed is good." Money and power are portrayed as the ultimate motives of human ambition and to think otherwise is portrayed as naïve. The narrative of people as greedy, money-hungry maximizers, or *homo economicus*, is dominant.[15]

Yet, there seems to be something wrong with the larger cultural narrative about what human beings value first and foremost. As the economist Richard Layard has said, there is something wrong when we have unprecedented material wealth and economic growth but stagnating levels of human well-being.[16] As Bob Chapman, the CEO of multi-billion-dollar manufacturing conglomerate Barry-Wehmiller, puts it, leaders are the problem not the solution to the current problems. The dominant narrative of business and success is failing. The cracks in our system are too obvious to ignore and require us to look at the foundations.

The experiences of Elisabeth, John, and Natalia showcase a reality and a background narrative that we label "economistic." The economistic narrative is based on axiomatic notions of who we are as people. It is not based on scientific insights but on assumptions that are exemplified by such fictional characters as Ebenezer Scrooge, Gordon Gekko, the Wolf of Wall Street, and in real life by such villains as Bernie Madoff. The narrative holds that people are fundamentally self-serving, looking for material wealth as an indicator of success. It is amoral in the sense that any behavior is acceptable as long as it helps to make more money. Other people are treated as a means to personal gain, and trickster behavior is considered sly, smart, and legitimate. The assumptions are simple and therefore very powerful.

---

[14] Bailey, C., & Madden, A. (2016). What makes work meaningful – or meaningless. *MIT Sloan Management Review, 57*(4), 53–61.

[15] Bregman, R. (2020). *Humankind: A hopeful history*. Bloomsbury Publishing.

[16] Layard, R., & De Neve, J. E. (2023). *Wellbeing*. Cambridge University Press.

At the core of the three life stories lies a narrative about business that is hostile to the "good life," as many people perceive it.[17] Changing the narrative is at the heart of a concerted effort to rethink how people have come to understand life and their role within the economic system. I argue that a change toward a humanistic paradigm will allow us to lead better lives, create business organizations that serve societal flourishing, and support a life-conducive economic system.

Signals of Crisis – Three Challenges to the Current System

In 2001, Kofi Annan, the late Secretary General of the United Nations, wisely predicted

> My friends, the simple fact of the matter is this: if we cannot make globalization work for all, in the end it will work for none. The unequal distribution of benefits, and the imbalances in global rule-making, which characterize globalization today, inevitably will produce backlash and protectionism. And that, in turn, threatens to undermine and ultimately to unravel the open world economy that has been so painstakingly constructed over the course of the past half-century.[18]

Years later, we know that his dire prediction came true. The so-called neoliberal consensus under which markets are the ultimate rationale of what is valuable has failed. According to scientific historian Thomas Kuhn, we are experiencing a paradigmatic crisis.[19]

Systemic Challenges

Symptoms of this paradigmatic breakdown are emerging across many levels. At the system level, scientists have long argued that we are overshooting the capacity of our planet to sustain our species and life in general. We are experiencing the sixth mass extinction, and biodiversity loss is rampant.[20] The effects of climate change on our health and well-being are becoming ever more obvious. Nature's ability to sustain our current way of

---

[17] Hunter Lovins, L. (2016). Needed: A better story. *Humanistic Management Journal, 1*(1), 75–90.

[18] Annan, K., & Secretary-General, U. (2001, January 29). *Address to the World Economic Forum: Secretary-General says globalization must work for all* (statement delivered in Davos, Switzerland, 28 January 2001). United Nations Department of Public Information, pp. 1–4. https://digitallibrary.un.org/record/432026

[19] Thomas, K. (1962). The structure of scientific revolutions. *International Encyclopedia of Unified Science, 2*(2), 1–172.

[20] Algeo, T. J., & Shen, J. (2024). Theory and classification of mass extinction causation. *National Science Review, 11*(1).

life is increasingly showing its limitations.[21] Humanity is using the productive capacity of more than 1.5 planets to satisfy its desires.[22] If everybody on this planet were to consume natural resources at the rate of an average American, five planets would be required.[23] In financial terms, humanity is living off its planetary capital and not the interest generated by it, which represents a poor management of resources.[24] This lack of sustainability is, however, supported by the logic of our current system. Shareholder capitalism is short-term oriented and, when applied rigorously, rewards plundering over preserving. As ecological economist Robert Costanza says, economics does not value the future.[25] In finance, one of the most central concepts is Net Present Value, which diminishes the value of the future.

The neoliberal system has lost its legitimacy in many places, including in the United States and the United Kingdom, which were its foremost champions. New levels of poverty and inequality post-COVID have brought about new resistance, destabilized long-standing democratic order, and ushered in new tribalist governments.

One-sixth of the world's population lives in extreme poverty.[26] Current trends in globalization have led to a world in which the rich get richer, and the poor get disproportionately poorer. Absolute poverty may have decreased in recent years, but relative poverty has increased sizeably.[27] Political unrest, collectivization, and terrorism are fed by such inequalities, which in turn require significant investments for the preservation of the status quo (e.g., through higher defense spending and corruption).[28]

---

21 Merz, J. J., Barnard, P., Rees, W. E., Smith, D., Maroni, M., Rhodes, C. J., Dederer, J. H., Bajaj, N., Joy, M. K., Wiedmann, T., & Sutherland, R. (2023). World scientists' warning: The behavioural crisis driving ecological overshoot. *Science Progress, 106*(3), 00368504231201372.

22 Aydin, M., Sogut, Y., & Altundemir, M. E. (2023). Moving toward the sustainable environment of European Union countries: Investigating the effect of natural resources and green budgeting on environmental quality. *Resources Policy, 83*, 103737. https://doi.org/10.1016/j.resourpol.2023.103737

23 Footprintnetwork. (2023, August 3). *How many Earths? How many countries? – Earth Overshoot Day.* Earth Overshoot Day. https://overshoot.footprintnetwork.org/how-many-earths-or-countries-do-we-need/

24 Victor, P. A. (2023). *Escape from overshoot: Economics for a planet in peril.* New Society Publishers.

25 Costanza, R. (2010). Toward a new sustainable economy. In S. Kates (Ed.), *Macroeconomic theory and its failings.* Edward Elgar Publishing.

26 Columbia Climate School the Earth Institute. (n.d.). *Extreme poverty: A global emergency.* Columbia Climate School the Earth Institute. Retrieved November 27, 2024, from www.earth.columbia.edu/articles/view/1780

27 Hasell, J., Roser, M., Ortiz-Ospina, E., & Arriagada, P. (2023, December 28). *Poverty. Our World in Data.* https://ourworldindata.org/poverty

28 Fukuyama, F. (2018). *Identity: The demand for dignity and the politics of resentment.* Farrar, Straus and Giroux.

Research increasingly shows the deleterious effects of inequality on human well-being, especially on health.[29] Shareholder capitalism is mostly blind to these consequences and has not yet provided satisfactory answers to deal with these issues. As sustainability scholars Paul Hawken, Amory Lovins, and Hunter Lovins have argued, economics does not value social relationships.[30]

Organizational-Level Challenges

Bob Chapman, CEO of Barry-Wehmiller, has called out his fellow leaders, accusing them of being the biggest threat to human health.[31] Jeffrey Pfeffer, the renowned business scholar, has demonstrated how people are impacted by bad business practices that lead to premature deaths across the globe.[32] Larry Fink, the large-scale investor and CEO of BlackRock, called on current CEOs to shift their way of doing business in order to become future proof.

Surveys indicate that stakeholder trust in businesses is decreasing dramatically, specifically in large global companies bent on shareholder value maximization. Trust is, however, commonly viewed as the key enabler for cooperation, motivation, and innovation, all of which are required to achieve an organization's peak performance and its eventual success. Research has found that the decline in trust is heavily correlated with a lack of value congruency between stakeholders and the organization.[33] Profit maximization goals are perceived as inherently opportunistic, which makes it ever more difficult for the business community to reestablish trust. My students are all jaded when it comes to studying business ethics because seemingly every day another scandal hits the newspapers, and most companies get away with a small fine.

As we have seen in the three examples given at the start of this section, employees are checking out of their organizations, and when not

---

[29] Wilkinson, R., & Pickett, K. (2011). *The spirit level: Why greater equality makes societies stronger*. Bloomsbury Publishing USA. Pickett, K. E., & Wilkinson, R. G. (2015). Income inequality and health: A causal review. *Social Science & Medicine, 128*, 316–326.

[30] Hawken, P., Lovins, A. B., & Lovins, L. H. (2013). *Natural capitalism: The next industrial revolution*. Routledge.

[31] Chapman, B., & Sisodia, R. (2015). *Everybody matters: The extraordinary power of caring for your people like family*. Portfolio. https://youtu.be/XLwS7vh9XbY

[32] Pfeffer, J. (2018). *Dying for a paycheck: How modern management harms employee health and company performance – and what we can do about it*. Harper Business.

[33] Pirson, M., & Malhotra, D. (2008). Unconventional insights for managing stakeholder trust. *MIT Sloan Management Review, 49*(4), 43–50.

"quietly quitting," they resign from within, doing minimal job duties to keep their paycheck. The "Great Resignation" following COVID only extended a trend that was long in the making. According to several Gallup studies before COVID, around 70 percent of US employees were either not engaged or actively disengaged, showing an alarming inner withdrawal rate.[34] Management scholar Michael Jensen argues that the goal of profit maximization is partially responsible for this. He posits it as self-evident that:

> Creating value takes more than acceptance of value maximization as the organizational objective. As a statement of corporate purpose or vision, value maximization is not likely to tap into the energy and enthusiasm of employees and managers to create value.[35]

Hence, shareholder value-maximizing organizations are underutilizing their employees' potential. Now, many corporate leaders see that, and many are talking about the importance of purpose at work. Somehow, for most employees this conversation only exacerbates their cynicism as they suspect "purpose washing."

Individual-Level Challenges

The symptoms of our current paradigm crisis show up in each of our lives with depression and increasing suicide rates.[36] The younger generation is experiencing unprecedented anxiety and they organize mass protests against climate change.[37] Scholars have long pointed out that the average level of life satisfaction has not increased despite there being more wealth for many. GDP growth and growth in well-being have decoupled.[38]

---

[34] Employee Engagement | Gallup Topic.

[35] Jensen, M. (2001). Value maximisation, stakeholder theory, and the corporate objective function. *European Financial Management*, 7(3), 297–317.

[36] Simon, D. H., & Masters, R. K. (2024). Institutional failures as structural determinants of suicide: The opioid epidemic and the Great Recession in the United States. *Journal of Health and Social Behavior*, 65(3), 415–431. https://doi.org/10.1177/00221465231223723
Glenn, C. R., Kleiman, E. M., Kellerman, J., Pollak, O., Cha, C. B., Esposito, E. C., Porter, A. C., Wyman, P. A., & Boatman, A. E. (2020). Annual research review: A meta-analytic review of worldwide suicide rates in adolescents. *Journal of Child Psychology and Psychiatry*, 61(3), 294–308.
Liu, Qingqing, He, H., Yang, Y., Feng, X., Zhao, F., & Lyu, J. (2020). Changes in the global burden of depression from 1990 to 2017: Findings from the Global Burden of Disease study. *Journal of Psychiatric Research*, 126, 134–140.

[37] Climate activists in Germany to abandon gluing themselves to streets, employ new tactics | *AP News* (accessed November 12, 2024).

[38] Easterlin, R. A. (2015). *Happiness and economic growth–the evidence* (pp. 283–299). Springer Netherlands.

Factors that contribute to well-being have a relatively low correlation with material wealth once a certain wealth level has been achieved.[39] On an individual level, the quality of social relationships, good physical and mental health, and a generally positive attitude toward life are central drivers of well-being. Materialism as an attitude, for example, turns out to be toxic for well-being.[40] Many studies show that a personal quest for more money or consumer goods decreases people's sense of personal well-being. As the writer and campaigner George Monbiot highlights:

> This is the dreadful mistake we are making: allowing ourselves to believe that having more money and more stuff enhances our wellbeing, a belief possessed not only by those poor deluded people in the pictures, but by almost every member of almost every government. Worldly ambition, material aspiration, perpetual growth: these are a formula for mass unhappiness.[41]

Conclusion

The current system is built on increases in consumption that lead to economic growth, yet it makes many people less happy with their lives. The advertising industry, for example, exists to create artificial material wants and is considered successful the more people try to feed their wants with more consumption, which drives up raw material use and creates all other kinds of related environmental and social problems. For societies that pride themselves on freedom of choice and democratic values, such unreflective practices undermine their very essence.

2 The Water We Swim In

> There are these two young fish swimming along and they happen to meet an older fish swimming the other way, who nods at them and says "Morning, boys. How's the water?" And the two young fish swim on for a bit, and then eventually one of them looks over at the other and goes "What the hell is water?"[42]

---

[39] Jebb, A. T., Tay, L., Diener, E., & Oishi, S. (2018). Happiness, income satiation and turning points around the world. *Nature Human Behaviour*, 2(1), 33–38. https://doi:10.1038/s41562-017-0277-0. Epub 2018 Jan 8. PMID: 30980059. Note: This finding has become more debated yet it seems clear that income does not produce well-being at the same rate as other sources.

[40] Pandelaere, M. (2016). Materialism and well-being: The role of consumption. *Current Opinion in Psychology*, 10, 33–38.

[41] Monbiot, G. (2017, November 30). Materialism: A system that eats us from the inside out. The Guardian. www.theguardian.com/commentisfree/2013/dec/09/materialism-system-eats-us-from-inside-out

[42] Foster., Wallace, David (2009). *This is water: Some thoughts, delivered on a significant occasion about living a compassionate life.* Kenyon College (1st ed.). Little, Brown.

As we are engaging in our daily relationships and navigating our organizational lives, we all employ a rule of thumb (heuristic) to how we assess ourselves and others. Oftentimes we are not aware of what our heuristics are, as they are subconscious and many times cultural. David Foster Wallace compares our cultural standards and subconsciousness as the water we swim in.

We take for granted the assumptions embedded in our cultures as well as the structure and patterns of our thinking and routines that envelop our being. The water we swim in is determined by how we view ourselves and others. One of the predominant narratives of who we are as human beings is exemplified by Gordon Gekko or Scrooge McDuck. We are fundamentally greedy, evil, and asocial. We are in it for ourselves only.

In Oliver Stone's hit movie of the 1980s, *Wall Street*, Michael Douglas stars as investment banker Gordon Gekko, who shares his philosophy of life and his notion of how the world works.

> Greed, for lack of a better word, is good. Greed is right, greed works. Greed clarifies, cuts through, and captures the essence of the evolutionary spirit. Greed, in all of its forms – greed for life, for money, for love, for knowledge – has marked the upward surge of mankind.[43]

In this assertion, Gordon Gekko formulates the neoliberal foundation of the economistic thinking that has permeated our culture.[44] The neoliberal narrative of who people are has deeply influenced culture and, we assert, has contributed to the pervasive cynicism with which many of us tend to explain human motivation. People are only self-interested, business is for crooks (business sucks), and we just have to accept it and suffer through it.[45]

It turns out this perspective is not only incorrect, it is fundamentally flawed and is endangering our own survival.[46] Using the current understanding of human beings, often referred to as homo economicus, we have "successfully" organized our world to best serve those that resemble most closely these psychopathic traits. While for some there is ever more wealth and increases in health and longevity,[47] those organizational efforts have

---

[43] Stone, Oliver. (1987). Wall Street, American Rhetoric: Movie Speech: Wall Street – Gordon Gekko Addresses Teldar Shareholders – Greed Is Good.

[44] Much of Sections 1 to 4 has been adapted from my prior writing, especially my 2017 book, "Humanistic Management: Protecting Dignity and Promoting Well-Being," published by Cambridge University.

[45] Bregman, R. (2020). *Humankind: A hopeful history*. Bloomsbury Publishing.

[46] Ibid.

[47] Deaton, A. (2024). *The great escape: Health, wealth, and the origins of inequality*. Princeton University Press.

also created increasing isolation, separation, and collective despera-
tion.[48,49] Although these kinds of observations are typically dismissed as
whimsical, soft, woo-woo, or socialist (especially in the United States), it
turns out they tell us something important about human nature that contradicts homo economicus assumptions.[50] We will turn to insights from
evolutionary biology in a moment to set us straight.[51]

Before we do that, it is imperative to understand the nature and size of
our task as leaders, organizers, managers, and human beings who care
about the state of the world, and, of course, for those who are naïve (or
realistic) enough, like Buckminster Fuller, to think we can create a world
that works for 100 percent of humanity.

One of the critical stepping stones to better management theory and
practice is a better and more accurate understanding of who we are as
people. The economistic narrative is based on assumptions that lead to a
reductionist model, which, in many ways, only describes deficient human
beings, such as psychopaths, sociopaths, or free riders – men and women
without morals.[52]

The REM Model

The most prominent articulation of human nature according to the economistic paradigm is that set forth by Michael Jensen and William Meckling,
two of the most prominent and oft-cited management scholars. Whereas
many researchers have memetically and unreflectedly adopted an economistic perspective, these scholars have specified their understanding of
human nature.

In their 1994 paper titled "The Nature of Man," they postulate that
understanding human behavior is fundamental to understanding how
organizations function, whether they are profit-making firms, nonprofit
enterprises, or government agencies.[53] They argue that their model,

---

[48] Richard, B. (2024). Why loneliness is bad for your health. *Nature, 628*, 23.

[49] Surgeon General: Our Loneliness Epidemic. Social connection can transform our whole
health and well-being. www.hhs.gov/surgeongeneral/priorities/connection/index.html

[50] Wilson, D. S., O'Brien, D. T., & Sesma, A. (2009). Human prosociality from an evolutionary perspective: Variation and correlations at a city-wide scale. *Evolution and Human
Behavior, 30*(3), 190–200.

[51] Lawrence, P. R. (2010). *Driven to lead: Good, bad, and misguided leadership* (Vol. 168).
John Wiley & Sons.

[52] Ibid.

[53] Jensen, M. C., & Meckling, W. H. (1994). The nature of man. *The Journal of Applied
Corporate Finance*, Summer, 4–19.

REMM – the Resourceful, Evaluative, Maximizing Model – is superior. Jensen and Meckling state that:

> [REMM] serves as the foundation for the agency model of financial, organizational, and governance structure of firms. The growing body of social science research on human behavior has a common message: Whether they are politicians, managers, academics, professionals, philanthropists, or factory workers, individuals are resourceful, evaluative maximizers.[54]

In turn, agency theory was hailed as a grand theory in the social sciences, influencing economics, management, sociology, and political science. As such, REMM held sway over a much larger part of social science than its design intended. The famed economist Harold Demsetz argued that economistic theoretical models are used to study human behavior in the marketplace.[55] They are therefore useful to help us understand the possibility of spontaneous order in this marketplace, but should not be seen as prescriptive tools with regard to other institutions, such as organizations or societies.[56]

Yet, this model, unbeknownst to most people, has become the water we swim in.[57] Jensen and Meckling's theorizing not only had an enormous impact on management theory but also on management practice. Based on their research on the theory of the firm, corporate governance was redesigned, motivational schemes were developed, and stock options were created. Harvard University's Rakesh Khurana describes an event in the early 1980s in which corporate raiders linked to T. Boone Pickens provided regulators with copies of Jensen and Meckling's papers when they needed to convince them that his proposed takeovers would be the best way to deliver shareholder value maximization.[58] Much as Gordon Gekko later described.

REMM Revisited

In this light, it is helpful to examine REMM and its intellectual arguments more closely. While we don't have much space to go into detail here,

---

[54] Ibid.

[55] Demsetz, H. (2011). *From economic man to economic system: Essays on human behavior and the institutions of capitalism.* Cambridge University Press.

[56] Ibid.
Rajan, R. (2019). *The third pillar: How markets and the state leave the community behind.* Penguin Press.

[57] Bregman, R. (2020). *Humankind: A hopeful history.* Bloomsbury Publishing.

[58] Khurana, R. (2010). *From higher aims to hired hands: The social transformation of American business schools and the unfulfilled promise of management as a profession.* Princeton University Press.

I have done so in prior writing.[59] In short, Jensen and Meckling suggested that REMM was the product of over 200 years of research and debate in economics, the other social sciences, and philosophy. They provided a number of postulates that served as a "bare bones summary of the concept."

The first postulate suggests that people continually evaluate and that we are willing to make tradeoffs constantly.[60] The biggest empirical problem is the assumption that human beings do not know commitments or that, in the end, we all behave opportunistically at all times.[61] This assumption does not allow for commitments such as marriage vows, relationships, or friendships, whose nature is not subject to barter or quid pro quo; while healthy community life, in which people support each other without taking potential payback into account (e.g., care for children, the elderly, and even dead ancestors), is unimaginable. This assumption contradicts evidence from evolutionary biology and anthropology, which claims that human survival depended on honoring social contracts and commitments through loyalty to the family and tribe.[62]

In a further postulate, Jensen and Meckling argue that there are no human *needs* as such, which cannot be exchanged, but only *wants* which can be exchanged.

> Like it or not, individuals are willing to sacrifice a little of almost anything we care to name, even reputation or morality, for a sufficiently large quantity of other desired things; and these things do not have to be money or even material goods.[63]

Henry Mintzberg paraphrases their postulate derisively by saying that accordingly we are "whores," selling anything and everything and honoring nothing.[64] This is factually inaccurate, even though it may be correct in certain situations.[65]

---

[59] Pirson, M. (2017). *Humanistic management: Protecting dignity and promoting well-being.* Cambridge University Press.

[60] Jensen, M. C., & Meckling, W. H. (1994). The nature of man. *The Journal of Applied Corporate Finance*, Summer, 4–19.

[61] Mintzberg, H. (2005). *Managers not MBAs.* Berrett Kohler Publishers.

[62] Wilson, E. O. (2012). *The social conquest of earth.* Liveright Publishing Corporation.

[63] Jensen, M. C., & Meckling, W. H. (1994). The nature of man. *The Journal of Applied Corporate Finance*, Summer, 4–19.

[64] Mintzberg, H. (2005). *Managers not MBAs.* Berrett Kohler Publishers.

[65] Sayer, A. (2011). *Why things matter to people: Social science, values and ethical life.* Cambridge University Press.

Research increasingly finds that moral judgments and value-based commitments are intrinsic elements of human sociality.[66] While the Jensen and Meckling's postulate postulate is certainly provocative and entertaining, the mere claim that humans have no needs does not make it so. From an evolutionary perspective, humans have developed basic needs that they cannot trade off if they are to survive.[67] Needs exist to the degree that they *must* be fulfilled, like eating or drinking, because without these survival is impossible. According to REMM assumptions, small babies will trade off their need for food to gain fame, for example. While eating is a need, fame is a want, and it is hard to credit that babies would prefer fame over food. While there are clearly extreme situations, for example, when people trade off their personal integrity for personal survival by prostituting themselves, those situations do not represent normal human behavior.[68]

Jensen and Meckling, however, build on this notion of wants in Postulate II:

> Each individual's wants are unlimited. (a) If we designate those things that REMM values positively as "goods," then he or she prefers more goods to less. Goods can be anything from art objects to ethical norms. (b) REMM cannot be satiated. He or she always wants more of some things, be they material goods such as art, sculpture, castles, and pyramids; or non-material goods such as solitude, companionship, honesty, respect, love, fame, and immortality.[69]

In this postulate, REMM shows its deep connection with the homo economicus model. REMM must have unlimited wants, otherwise the maximization of utility cannot make sense. While Jensen and Meckling attempt to broaden the realm of "goods" from the purely material to the ideal, REMM is simply homo economicus reborn and attempting to maximize.

Research in psychology and neuroscience challenges the belief that the human urge to satisfy wants is unlimited.[70] Increasing evidence shows that

---

[66] Kahneman, D. (2011). *Fast and slow thinking*. Allen Lane and Penguin Books.
Roach, S. C. (2016). Why moral commitments matter: Mapping the ethics and politics of responsible and accountable global governance. *Cambridge Review of International Affairs*, *29*(1), 309–326.

[67] Wilson, D. S. (2007). *Evolution for everyone: How Darwin's theory can change the way we think about our lives*. Delta.

[68] Bregman, R. (2020). *Humankind: A hopeful history*. Bloomsbury Publishing.
Davidson, J. O. C. (1998). *Prostitution, power, and freedom*. University of Michigan Press.

[69] Jensen, M. C., & Meckling, W. H. (1994). The nature of man. *The Journal of Applied Corporate Finance*, Summer, 4–19.

[70] Schwartz, B. (2004). The tyranny of choice. *Scientific American*, *290*(4), 70–75.

wanting less can be healthy,[71] and that an increasing number of young people reject the notion that more is better. Pursuing unlimited wants may be burdening and troublesome.[72] "Affluenza," the description of the consistent pursuit of more, is considered a modern disease.[73] According to REMM, affluenza should not exist; given that humans inherently want more, there can be no satiation. Not only does recent psychological evidence contradict this assumption, but also the global religious traditions have long suggested that wisdom starts with the recognition that there is such a thing as "enough."[74]

Similarly, psychology finds that people are happiest if they commit to a limited amount of choices.[75] For example, people with one spouse and who are able to grow in that relationship are happier than those who are promiscuous.[76] Evolutionary biology, which finds that most humans desire to have a nuclear family, supports this finding.[77] While not always practically possible, a stable relationship increases the survival chances of healthy offspring.[78] If people acted according to REMM, they would desire an unlimited number of partners.

Jensen and Meckling build on the notion of unlimited *wants* with Postulate III and IV where they add that we are not static maximizers but creative and resourceful in how we maximize. While I go into more detail in my prior book,[79] for now I will conclude my assessment of their model of human nature with the following comparison.

To take their perspective to its logical conclusion, let's consider the example of Elisabeth. Elisabeth is a mother of two kids, married to a

---

[71] Seligman, M. (2002). *Authentic happiness: Using the new positive psychology to realize your potential to lasting fulfillment*. The Free Press. Gilbert, D. (2009). *Stumbling on happiness*. Vintage Canada. Lyubomirsky, S. (2007). *The how of happiness: A scientific approach to getting the life you want*. Penguin Press.

[72] http://elitedaily.com/life/culture/millennials-minimalists/1256085/ (accessed October 14, 2024).

[73] See, for example, www.psychologytoday.com/blog/feeling-our-way/201602/the-affluenza-defense
De Graaf, J., Wann, D., & Naylor, T. H. (2014). *Affluenza: How overconsumption is killing us – and how to fight back*. Berrett-Koehler Publishers.

[74] Küng, H. (1998). *A global ethic for global politics and economics*. Oxford University Press. Smith, H. (1985). *Forgotten truth: The common vision of the world's religions*. HarperOne.

[75] Gilbert, D. (2009). *Stumbling on happiness*. Vintage Canada. Lama, D., & Cutler, H. C. (2003). *The art of happiness at work*. Riverhead Books. Lyubomirsky, S. (2007). *The how of happiness: A scientific approach to getting the life you want*. Penguin Press.

[76] Lyubomirsky, S. (2007). *The how of happiness: A scientific approach to getting the life you want*. Penguin Press.

[77] Wrangham, R. W. (2009). *Catching fire: How cooking made us human*. Basic Books.

[78] Wilson, E. O. (2012). *The social conquest of earth*. Liveright Publishing Corporation. Wrangham, R. W. (2009). *Catching fire: How cooking made us human*. Basic Books.

[79] Pirson, M. (2017). *Humanistic management: Protecting dignity and promoting well-being*. Cambridge University Press.

husband who has to travel for his work very often. She works in hospital administration and also needs to take care of her mother who lives in the area. Her wish to be successful at her job, have a good relationship with her spouse, provide a good education for her kids, and take care of her mother's needs defines her opportunity set. The REMM-type Elisabeth could use her ingenuity to create a life situation in which she decides to maximize all of these ambitions. Wanting to be successful at her job, she would need to spend more time and energy at the hospital. Because she hardly sees her husband, she decides (knowing no commitments and willing to substitute anything) to divorce her husband and marry her boss. At the hospital, they can spend more time together, while increasing her income. The additional income could be used to pay a tutor for her kids, allowing her to outsource their education. As she spends so much time at work, she ingeniously suggests to her mother that she should (pretend to) become ill, which will mean that she too can be at the hospital. While such behavior may be ingenious and creative, it is also rather absurd. It is far more likely that Elisabeth will simply decide to spend just enough time at the hospital to ensure she does not lose her job, spend quality time with her current husband and not get divorced, take care of her kids when she can in order to personally provide educational experiences, and to look after her mother in her home when she is able to. In the latter case, Elisabeth is balancing creatively rather than ingeniously maximizing options within her opportunity set.

It is important to note that Jensen and Meckling never strive for an accurate model, but simply for a better model than that of homo economicus. Many of their assumptions are partially true, and they expend much energy in demonstrating their postulations' validity in and beyond economics and management literature. The philosopher Karl Popper would, however, call many of these efforts "verificationism," which he describes as the tendency to explain reality with the set of assumptions we create.[80] Consequently, when studying human organizing practices, researchers tend to make reality fit their assumptions, rather than the inverse.

Evolutionary Biology to the Rescue

It turns out that we as a human species have survived because we are fundamentally able to balance several key drives – not maximize any of them (more on this later).[81] Also, our hominoid ancestors from 1.8 million years ago

---

[80] Popper, K. (2005). *The logic of scientific discovery*. Routledge.

[81] Lawrence, P. R. (2010). *Driven to lead: Good, bad, and misguided leadership* (Vol. 168). John Wiley & Sons.

became fundamentally social as a key strategy to collaborate and survive.[82] This may sound perplexing, but consider how important families are to our species' survival, and how, despite all the problems, we seem to follow basic rules of respect and give and take. In fact, we have a term for people that do not have families (adoptive/foster or natural) or other social support systems (such as orphanages). EXTINCT…

Paul Lawrence of Harvard collected the evidence provided by evolutionary biology and reread the original Darwin (*Descent of Man*) and suggested that we have survived because we have four independent drives that constitute homo sapiens: The drive to *acquire* what we need to survive, the drive to *defend* that which we need to survive, the drive to *bond* with other human beings, and the drive to *comprehend* the world around us.[83]

We will look at the evidence for the drive to bond and drive to comprehend later. For now, the argument is that we need to balance those four drives. Every time we have tried to maximize one of them, our species has created deadly conflict and undermined its survival (see Section 5).

Conclusion

The economistic worldview has a stranglehold over our culture and informs our view of management. REMM is supporting business education and legitimizes asocial behavior. If we want to manage better, we need a better understanding of who we are as people. Sounds simple and is challenging. Luckily, scientific progress can help us.

3 Revisiting Human Nature

Perhaps most people, including many scholars, would like to keep human nature at least partly in the dark. It is the monster in the fever swamp of public discourse. Its perception is distorted by idiosyncratic personal self-regard and expectation. Economists have by and large steered around it, while philosophers bold enough to search for it always lost their way. Theologians tend to give up, attributing different parts to God and the devil. Political ideologues ranging from anarchists to fascists have defined it to their selfish advantage.[84]

---

[82] Wilson, E. O. (2012). *The social conquest of earth*. Liveright Publishing Corporation.

[83] Lawrence, P. R. (2010). *Driven to lead: Good, bad, and misguided leadership* (Vol. 168). John Wiley & Sons. Lawrence, P. R., & Pirson, M. (2015). Economistic and humanistic narratives of leadership in the age of globality: Toward a renewed Darwinian theory of leadership. *Journal of Business Ethics, 128*, 383–394.

[84] Wilson, E. O. (2012). *On human nature*. Harvard University Press.

Examining human nature as such has become a dirty endeavor. Many philosophers and ethicists deem it an unimportant question, others are afraid of the political implications, and, indeed, many scholars who have raised this question got into a lot of trouble in the past – with good reason, the answers provided often looked like they determined a certain type of human behavior as well as prescribing some public policy that was not supportive to overall human flourishing.[85] And while the conversation and debate about human nature – or who we are – is never going to lose its controversial power, it is important to revisit the emerging insights against the backdrop of the polycrisis.[86]

As we have seen, the economistic worldview which underlies the dominant form of organizing business is powerful and rests on assumptions, not necessarily on facts. Because it is inaccurate, we are experiencing huge dissatisfaction with our organizations. Hence, we need to revisit other potential perspectives on human nature that will support more life-conducive management.

We saw in Section 2 that every model of human behavior needs to trade off parsimony for accuracy. REMM, for example, loosens many restrictive assumptions about homo economicus to gain accuracy. The model was never designed to be perfect, however, and there may be alternative and better ways to conceptualize human nature.

In the following sections, other perspectives seeking to understand human nature provide a counterpoint to REMM. The famed biologist E. O. Wilson suggests that there seems to be a consilience of knowledge in which core insights from the sciences overlap with those of the humanities.[87] These insights can help us understand human nature better. This increasing consilience of knowledge can serve as a stepping stone to better management.

Sociality

Referring to biology and evolutionary theory, Wilson argues that inherited regularities in the mental development common to our species define human nature.[88] Nevertheless, he suggests that our "epigenetic rules,"

---

[85] Much of Sections 1 to 4 has been adapted from my prior writing, especially my 2017 book "Humanistic Management: Protecting Dignity and Promoting Well-Being," published by Cambridge University.

[86] Henig, D., & Knight, D. M. (2023). Polycrisis: Prompts for an emerging worldview. *Anthropology Today*, *39*(2), 3–6.

[87] Wilson, E. O. (1998). *Consilience: The unity of knowledge*. Alfred A. Knopf.

[88] Wilson, E. O. (2012). *On human nature*. Harvard University Press.

which have evolved through the interaction of individual and group selection mechanisms, define us. Homo sapiens is therefore a result of an interplay between a genetic and a cultural evolution that occurred over a long period and started in deep prehistory. Wilson specifies that the hardwired epigenetic rules are the core of human nature. These epigenetic rules create the resulting behaviors common to homo sapiens. That means that the behaviors are "prepared" and ready to be developed, but need to be learned. That is why education and socialization are critical for human survival.

Supporting this proposition, George Murdock (1945) combed through human behaviors shared by many hundreds of societies, as studied by anthropologists in the past.[89] Murdock attempted to highlight cultural practices that are almost universal. A selection of these practices featuring human nature's eusocial character includes community organization, cooperative labor, courtship, dancing, decorative art, division of labor, education, ethics, faith healing, family feasting, food taboos, funeral rites, games, gift giving, government, hospitality, incest taboos, inheritance rules, joking, kin groups, kin nomenclature, marriage, mealtimes, postnatal care, property rights, religious ritual, sexual restriction, soul concepts, status differentiation, and the list goes on.

Other phenomena also bear witness to our eusocial nature. Why would inventions like the internet, cell phones, or Facebook make any sense, or have any commercial value, if we were not fundamentally social? The fundamental need – Paul Lawrence calls it the "drive to bond" – is hardwired; it serves an evolutionary purpose, which is the survival of the species rather than individual utility maximization.[90]

Morality

If we are fundamentally social, this may mean that we are also fundamentally moral. Joshua Greene, a noted scholar whose work bridges various disciplines in a true humanist fashion, writes: "Under ordinary circumstances, we shudder at the thought of behaving violently toward innocent people, even total strangers, and this most likely is a crucial feature of our moral brains."[91] Greene says that, in sum, we are a caring species, albeit

---

[89] Murdock, G. P. (1945). The common denominator of cultures. In R. Linton (Ed.), *The science of man in the world crisis* (pp. 123–142). Columbia University Press.

[90] Lawrence, P. (2010). *Driven to lead: Good, bad, and misguided leadership.* Jossey-Bass.

[91] Greene, J. (2014). *Moral tribes: Emotion, reason and the gap between us and them.* Atlantic Books Ltd.

in a limited way, and we probably inherited at least some of our caring capacity from our primate ancestors, if not our more distant ancestors. We care most of all about our relatives and friends, but we also care about acquaintances and strangers.

Robert Wright argues in the same vein and suggests humans are moral animals.[92] Both Wright and Greene suggest we have a moral machinery in our brain originating from our hypersocial nature. Joshua Greene writes: "From simple cells to supersocial animals like us, the story of life on Earth is the story of increasingly complex cooperation. Cooperation is why we are here, and yet at the same time, maintaining cooperation is our greatest challenge."[93] Morality is the human brain's answer to this challenge. Such morality is derived from emotional baseline responses, and Greene argues that for each cooperative strategy, our moral brains have a corresponding set of emotional dispositions that execute this strategy. Such strategies include concern for others, direct and indirect reciprocity, commitment to threats and promises, and reputation.

All of this psychological machinery is perfectly designed to promote cooperation among otherwise selfish individuals, implementing strategies that can be formalized in abstract mathematical terms. The additional insight that Greene and his collaborators present is that human morality and, as a result, cooperation are typically intuitive, not calculated or rational. Greene and his colleagues conducted experiments in which responses that required moral decision-making and cooperation choices were timed. Their results demonstrated that cooperative choices were made so fast that they had to be intuitive.

E. O. Wilson writes that morality, conformity, religious fervor, and fighting ability, combined with imagination and memory, produced homo sapiens as a winner in terms of survival.[94]

Empathy and Emotionality

Frans de Waal, a leading primatologist, writes that empathy is hardwired and that the emotional basis of empathy is critical for our sociality.[95] We cannot live peacefully in families, communities, and tribes without having

---

[92] Wright, R. (2010). *The moral animal: Why we are, the way we are: The new science of evolutionary psychology.* Vintage.

[93] Greene, J. (2014). *Moral tribes: Emotion, reason and the gap between us and them.* Atlantic Books Ltd. (p. 61).

[94] Wilson, E. O. (2012). *The social conquest of earth.* W. W. Norton & Company.

[95] Waal, F. B. M. d. (2009). *The age of empathy: Nature's lessons for a kinder society.* Harmony Books.

the tools to do so. Contrary to the Hobbesian, Spencerian, and Randian notion of human nature, homo sapiens is alive today because we care. De Waal and others find that empathy is, in many ways, a key lever to collaboration and can turn self-interest into mutual interest. In fact, Eric Liu and Nick Hanauer state that, through empathy, humans experience "true self-interest as mutual interest."[96]

De Waal and others argue that humans are not even that special in terms of empathetic abilities, but that animals of all kinds are capable of empathy and collaboration. Charles Darwin early on suggested that hardwired emotions representing the core of human nature drive such empathy. In *The Expression of the Emotions in Man and Animals*, Darwin suggests that empathetic instincts must have evolved from natural selection. E. O. Wilson argues that humans are fundamentally emotional beings because these emotions aided survival and reproduction. David Matsumoto writes that:

> ...emotions humans experience today emerged (or were naturally selected) in our evolutionary history as rapid information processing systems that helped us deal with the environment and events that occurred. That is, emotions evolved to help us cope with events and situations that had consequences for our immediate welfare. If humans didn't have emotions, we wouldn't know when to attack, defend, flee, care for others, reject food, or approach something useful, all of which were helpful in our evolutionary histories (as they are today). If we didn't feel disgusted at spoilt food, we would eat it. If we weren't outraged when rivals stole our food, resources, or mates, we wouldn't defend them strongly. If we didn't feel the joy in caring for a child, or the compassion in caring for a loved one, we wouldn't enjoy the social bonds that make human cultures and relationships unique.[97]

Joshua Greene and others suggest that empathy and our collaborative tendencies are instinctive and emotion-based. Frans de Waal calls it the "feeling brain," arguing that the basis of our emotional sensors is hard-coded in our brains. Emotions are a feature, not a bug. Emotions help us deal with the complexity of our eusocial life.

Basic emotions that can be witnessed across different cultures, and thus hint at their universality, include anger, contempt, disgust, fear, enjoyment, sadness, and surprise. These emotions are called basic because they

---

96 Hanauer, E. L. N. (2018, May 4). *Traditional Economics Failed. Here's a New Blueprint.* Evonomics. http://evonomics.com/traditional-economics-failed-heres-a-new-blueprint/

97 Matsumoto, D., San Francisco State University, & National Geographic Science (Spain). (n.d.). The origin of universal human emotions. In *National Geographic Science (Spain)* [Journal-article]. https://davidmatsumoto.com/content/NG%20Spain%20Article_2_.pdf

are shared across a number of species, including our primate ancestors. This fundamental emotionality challenges the uniquely rational focus of Jensen and Meckling's REMM propositions. Emotions also call into question theories of human behavior that are purely based on rationality, such as rational choice and decision-making.

Altruism

Eusociality and its derivatives – morality and baseline empathy supported by emotions – lead to human behavior that further questions REMM's basic assumptions regarding the maximization of self-interest. Altruism can be understood as an individual's behavior that benefits other individuals, even though these actions may negatively impact the individual's chances of survival. A well-known example is that of individuals who watch out for a predator and signal danger to the group, thus potentially drawing the predator's attention to themselves. The role of fairness and the development of altruistic punishment to uphold the tribe's moral rules have been documented in various studies. Altruism has been actively studied in fields as varied as biology, economics, sociology, and game theory. It differs from cooperation, as altruism requires no direct benefit or reciprocity. Studies show that *without* the emergence of altruism, populations go extinct. Emerging research suggests that altruism is a behavior common to the human species because group selection favored those groups with altruists over those without.

David Sloan Wilson summarizes the research as: "Selfishness beats altruism within groups. Altruistic groups beat selfish groups. Everything else is commentary."[98] Selfish behavior is found to undermine communities and leads to trouble for the group. For communities that survive, E. O. Wilson argues, the countervailing forces of altruism evolve through group selection, not just through individual selection.[99] It appears that a group-based selection mechanism screens for altruism. As such, altruism is now viewed as a key feature of functioning human groups.

Taken together, the findings from the natural sciences concerning human nature provide a clearer perspective on who we are as human beings. A number of elements long considered bugs in our system have now been identified as features, including sociality, morality, emotionality,

---

98 Wilson, D. S., & Wilson, E. O. (2007). Rethinking the theoretical foundation of sociobiology. *The Quarterly Review of Biology, 82*(4), 327–348.

99 Wilson, E. O. (2012). *On human nature.* Harvard University Press.

and altruism. These insights challenge REMM's claims about the nature of man that underlie a larger, dominant theoretical framework in management sciences.

Toward a Consilience of Knowledge on Human Nature

Many of the insights that now have increasing scientific backing were developed over time in the humanities. As early as Aristotle, philosophers suggested that human beings are social animals endowed with reason. In *The Human Condition*, Hanna Arendt writes that, basically, we are Aristotelian, political, social animals who crave meaning, and that this craving is often channeled into work and action as manifestations of our existence.[100] The sociality of human beings has rarely been called into question, even though the special role of human freedom and individual uniqueness has become more pronounced in modern Western thought. During the Enlightenment, philosophers established a convincing argument that although tribal, human nature requires special respect. The notion of human rights was born with the Kantian notion of the unconditional dignity of human nature. These human rights, based on the unconditional notion of human dignity, are sometimes viewed as commitments that are not negotiable. As such, they should escape the economistic exchange logic (at least in theory and as an aspiration). The economistic argument that they do not should thus be viewed with skepticism in light of the much longer philosophical tradition.

In line with Darwin's observation that morality must have developed as a survival mechanism for humanity, scholars of religion and ethics have identified the principles of such shared morality, or ethics, in order to develop a global, universal ethos that can help build bridges between religions and secular people. The noted psychologist Steven Pinker suggests:

> ... this foundation of morality may be seen in the many versions of the Golden Rule that have been discovered by the world's major religions, and also in Spinoza's Viewpoint of Eternity, Kant's Categorical Imperative, Hobbes' and Rousseau's Social Contract, and Locke and Jefferson's self-evident truth that all people are created equal.[101]

The Swiss theologian Hans Kueng and his collaborators studied the leading global religious and secular groups' narratives and suggested that we can find insights into our shared, universal human nature in the respective

---

[100] Arendt, H. (2013). *The human condition*. University of Chicago Press.
[101] www.nybooks.com/articles/2016/04/07/moral-psychology-an-exchange/

sacred texts' aspirational statements.[102] Many religions have clear guiding principles in terms of how human beings should behave. Some sort of universalist *ultima ratio*, which holds against all human instincts of self-preservation, supports these principles. Many anthropologists make the case that religion and creation narratives, which include rules for altruistic acts, are crucial for building a functioning society. An example of this is the narrative of Jesus Christ. While such narratives may be dismissed, they seem to have spoken to humans throughout the ages. As such, they may give a glimpse into true and persisting human needs and human nature.

Hans Kueng and his team suggest that secular and religious narratives have many elements in common. First, in the face of self-interest, they all assume that anyone who truly believes [in God, reincarnation, etc.] should in "practice consistently be concerned with human well-being." Kueng mentions the "twofold Jewish commandment to love God and one's neighbor and its further development in Jesus' Sermon on the Mount along with the incessant demand of the Qu'ran for justice, truth and good works; [...] the Buddhist doctrine of overcoming human suffering, the Hindu striving to fulfill 'dharma' and Confucius' requirement to preserve cosmic order and thus the humanum" to highlight the religious depth of human dignity as a basic principle and to indicate human well-being as the goal of human ethics.[103]

Furthermore, Kueng argues that despite their particularisms, all the great religions call for particular "non-negotiable standards, basic ethical norms and maxims to ensure basic humanity."

Kueng presents five universally shared commands across all the great world religions:

1. Do not kill
2. Do not lie
3. Do not steal
4. Do not practice immorality
5. Respect parents and love children.

He argues that such norms were possibly conceived as protection against unprincipled libertinism, which prioritizes personal advantage in the short run. In this sense, it could be argued that the great religions share principles

---

[102] Kueng, H., & Kuschel, K. J. (eds.). (1993). *Global ethic: The declaration of the parliament of the world's religions*. Bloomsbury Publishing. Kung, H. (2004). *Global responsibility: In search of a new world ethic*. Wipf and Stock Publishers.

[103] Ibid.

that protect humanity from REMM-style behavior fixated on wants that can be exchanged at liberty.

On the other hand, Kueng makes the argument that, ultimately, in order to promote human well-being, the great world religions straddle the extremes of libertinism and legalism, offering individuals a middle way (the Commandments are guides for human behavior, not binding laws). In this sense, the Golden Rule emerges as a guide for humans to live a "good life." Kueng provides evidence that long before Kant specified his categorical imperative, Confucius (551–489 BCE) had written: "What you yourself do not want, do not do to another person"; Rabbi Hillel (60 BCE–10 CE) similarly states: "Do not do to others what you would not want them to do to you"; while the Christian Bible specifies: "Whatever you want people to do to you do also to them" (Matthew 7.12; Luke 6.31).

Such moral motivations and guidelines are presented in the context of the lives of real people, be they prophets, saints, or spiritual leaders such as the Buddha, Confucius, Lao-tze, Jesus Christ, or Mohammed, and not in the abstract. The religious stories that are told are cultural narratives that provide practical guidance and, above all, meaning. In his book *Antifragile*, Nassim Taleb suggests that religious institutions are pretty stable.[104] This means they can tell us what has mattered to human beings throughout their existence. The shared principles of the global religions could therefore provide significant insights into human nature over time. These insights are a substantial challenge to REMM.

Human Nature: A View from the Social Sciences

The various domains of the social sciences have seen a number of developments rooted in a more humanistic, all-encompassing understanding of human nature. For example, Amartya Sen and his philosopher colleague Martha Nussbaum have provided a framework for a humanistic interpretation of economics.[105] Their capability approach is based on the assumptions of human dignity as unconditional and the presupposition that economic affairs ought to be managed to expand freedom and the capabilities of individuals to achieve a higher level of well-being. Other noted economists have defied economistic orthodoxy and expanded our view of human nature. Daniel Kahneman earned his Nobel Prize in economics by debunking the foundations of homo economicus. He calls the assumptions

---

[104] Taleb, N. N. (2012). *Antifragile: Things that gain from disorder* (Vol. 3). Random House Incorporated.

[105] Sen, A. (2001). *Development as freedom*. Oxford University Press.

of economic theory a "non-starter."[106] Elinor Ostrom received her Nobel Prize for defying homo economicus assumptions of pure self-interest. Ostrom is known to have not worked from theory, but from studying practice, which suggests that what works for practice should work for theory.

Ostrom's eight design principles of stable, local, common-pool resource management suggest that communities can manage the commons effectively and sustainably to advance the common good by means of:

1. Clearly defined boundaries (a clear definition of the contents of the common-pool resource and effective exclusion of external unentitled parties);
2. Rules regarding the appropriation and provision of common resources adapted to local conditions;
3. Collective-choice arrangements that allow most resource appropriators to participate in the decision-making process;
4. Effective monitoring by monitors who are part of, or accountable to, the appropriators;
5. A scale of graduated sanctions for resource appropriators who violate community rules;
6. Conflict-resolution mechanisms that are cheap and easy to access;
7. Higher-level authorities who acknowledge the community's self-determination; and
8. Organization in the form of multiple layers of nested enterprises, with small local CPRs at the base level, in the case of larger common-pool resources.[107]

A group of researchers associated with David Sloan Wilson studied the work of anthropologists to suggest that almost all hunter-gatherer societies that still exist, or which anthropologists described prior to their assimilation into larger societies, exhibit teamwork enforced by the suppression of disruptive self-serving behaviors. Bullying is not tolerated. The group as a whole has the power to thwart those who try to impose their will by creating counter-dominant coalitions. Status must be earned, and reputation is based on how much one contributes to the group. Decision-making is typically done by means of consensus or by other processes that the group recognizes as fair. It is easy to monitor agreed-upon behaviors, because

---

[106] Kahneman, D. (2007). "Judgment and Intuition." 2008 Distinguished Lecture Series sponsored by Harvard's Mind/Brain/Behavior (MBB) Interfaculty Initiative (MBB).

[107] Ostrom, E. (2009). *Design principles of robust property-rights institutions: What have we learned? Property rights and land policies.* K. Gregory Ingram & Yu-Hung Hong (Eds.). Lincoln Institute of Land Policy.

people are almost always in the presence of others. Mild sanctions, such as gossip, are usually sufficient to keep people in solid citizen mode, but these are backed up by harsher sanctions, such as exclusion and execution. Conflicts of interest are usually managed in a way that all the parties recognize as fair.

In a similar way, Wilson and colleagues studied the emergence and resilience of 1,400 business corporations. They found that the same principles hold. Human beings in these organizations constantly defy REMM's basic assumptions, leading the researchers to conclude:

> A theory is only as good as its assumptions and orthodox economic theory is a case of "garbage in, garbage out." Homo economicus and its imaginary social environment are such a far cry from Homo sapiens and real social environments that there is no theoretical justification for the orthodox school of thought. The argument that the predictions of a theory can be right even though its assumptions are wrong, which was advanced by Milton Friedman in the 1950s, sounds silly after the failure of orthodox economics to predict or cope with the economic crises facing us today. Very simply, the orthodox school of economics is an emperor with no clothes and the sooner this is widely appreciated the better.[108]

Referring to the vast literature in sociology, Wilson et al. conclude that our species is genetically adapted to implement the core design principles in small groups, confirming the thoughts of nineteenth-century French social theorist Alexis de Tocqueville: "The village or township is the only association which is so perfectly natural that, wherever a number of men are collected, it seems to constitute itself."[109]

In psychology, a number of scholars have explored the elements of human dignity and the notion of human flourishing. Primarily based on the work of Carl Rogers, humanist psychologists such as Frederick Herzberg and Abraham Maslow built on an expanded notion of human nature, inspiring what is currently labeled "Positive Psychology." This branch of psychology, which has recently spun off positive organizational behavior and positive organizational scholarship as correlates to the Organizational Sciences, also challenges REMM's baseline assumptions. Jonathan Haidt, for example, has even suggested that psychologists

---

[108] Wilson, D. S. et al. Doing well by doing good: An evolution institute report on socially responsible businesses. https://evolution-institute.org/

[109] De Tocqueville, A. (2003). *Democracy in America* (Vol. 10). Regnery Publishing. Wilson, D. S. et al. Doing well by doing good: An evolution institute report on socially responsible businesses. https://evolution-institute.org/

should reject pervasive methodological individualism and study what he calls "Hive Psychology."[110] As such, the social sciences as a whole could benefit from a more accurate perspective that reflects the eusocial nature of human beings.

Insights from psychology are also important for an understanding of the darker side of human nature. Clearly, as E. O. Wilson suggests, the epigenetic makeup of human nature balances the outcomes of individual and group selection.[111] In many functioning groups, disruptive self-serving behaviors and their underlying psychological impulses are only suppressed, not eliminated, and are ready to surface whenever opportunities allow. David Sloan Wilson likens humans to Dr. Jekyll and Mr. Hyde, combined in a single person.[112] To some extent, REMM exists in all humans, but culture, civilization, and education are designed to counter REMM-style characteristics and produce the eusocial part that allowed the survival of the species. Only the economistic model's recent ascendency has elevated mankind's antisocial tendencies to a virtue.

Conclusion

While this is a very selective set of findings, and many more disciplines could be drawn on to present a fuller picture of human nature, the main point is to highlight the consilience of scientific insights that now exists and the extent to which it contradicts the prevalently held view of human nature. Human beings have survived because they are truly social beings, for better or worse. As such, they have developed a way to keep their basic emotions in check by developing their brain (i.e., prefrontal cortex) and developed morality as a set of guidelines for general survival in communities and societies. These moral guidelines require commitments beyond libertine pleasure-seeking in the moment. They allow human beings to foresee conflicts and build lasting relationships. To build environments where human beings can flourish, a dignity threshold (meeting basic needs) needs to be established. When humans can build capabilities to develop themselves and their communities to achieve higher levels of well-being, they create the conditions for flourishing.

---

[110] Haidt, J., Seder, J. P., & Kesebir, S. (2008). Hive psychology, happiness, and public policy. *The Journal of Legal Studies, 37*(S2), S133–S156.

[111] Wilson, E. O. (2012). *On human nature.* Harvard University Press.

[112] Wilson, D. S. et al. Doing well by doing good: An evolution institute report on socially responsible businesses. https://evolution-institute.org/

These various insights allow us to recalibrate claims made by economists, which have been widely adopted in management science. The currently dominant narrative of homo economicus, or its successor REMM, overlooks important qualities of human nature that need to be revisited in a number of ways to enhance theorizing.

- First, humans are fundamentally social (eusocial),
- Second, they are fundamentally emotionally driven, which enhances survival,
- Third, reason and rationality act as a guide, but are not exclusively in charge of decision-making,
- Fourth, morality and ethical standards/commitments are crucial for eusocial beings,
- Fifth, altruistic behavior makes sense in the context of group survival norms that interplay with individual survival norms, and
- Sixth, commitments such as unconditional respect for human dignity and the aspiration to promote human well-being are critical for good communities (eusocial beings).

Humans have needs – emotional needs, social needs, and individual needs – in order to live a life in dignity. We also have needs and, quite clearly, wants which allow us to flourish. Moral and ethical commitments are critical for survival and are not just part of a trade/exchange. These insights allow us to present a solid theoretical alternative to REMM, which will be described in the following section.

4 A New Humanistic Model

> The most exciting breakthrough of the twenty-first century will not occur because of technology, but of an expanding concept of what it means to be human.[113]

In this section, I propose a new humanistic perspective on human nature capable of undergirding a life-conducive form of management theory and practice. Compared to REMM, the power of such a humanistic model is arguably twofold: it increases accuracy and it remains equally parsimonious. It also explains behavior that REMM models explain, but can go beyond this. It is not a naïve rejection of the evil in human nature, but

---

[113] Naisbitt, J. (1982). Megatrends. *New York*, *17*, 1982.

presents a comprehensive perspective that can explain good, collaborative, moral, and empathetic behavior, as well as evil, psychopathic, immoral behavior. It is thus more realistic.[114]

Basic Considerations

Before detailing the model, it is important to take a step back to situate the emergence of this novel humanistic perspective. Whereas economistic and humanistic conceptions have been presented as competing, it is critical to understand that they share a common origin. The German philosopher and former German Minister for Culture, Julian Nida-Ruemelin, argues that humanistic and economistic perspectives build on the assumption of human freedom and take the human individual as its starting point. Both perspectives are therefore equally hostile to any form of tribalism or collectivism as is now emerging on the global stage. Similarly, both traditions emphasize the human capacity for reasoning. As a result, homo economicus and REMM models can be helpful when examining market behavior based on individual reasoning.

The humanistic model builds on the old model, but expands it significantly by integrating insights from evolutionary science and the humanities. In contrast to economism, humanism, for example, assumes that human nature is not entirely a given, that it can be refined through education and learning. Universities and public schools were established under the auspices of the humanist tradition to form citizens. Similarly, Nida-Ruemelin suggests that another distinctive feature of humanism is the normative, ethical component that attributes unalienable rights to everybody, independent of ethnicity, nationality, social status, or gender. This view is echoed by other scholars, who propose the notion of *human dignity* as a baseline concept of humanistic thought. A dignity threshold is thus a universal baseline for the accordance of human rights for everyone.

Evolutionary biology increasingly supports the traditional humanistic perspective on human nature as a *zoon politikon*, a relational human being. According to the humanistic perspective, people materialize their freedom through value-based social interactions. When they engage well with people, they do so by protecting and enhancing their respective humanity and dignity; guided by the Golden Rule, they treat each other not only as a

---

[114] Much of Sections 1 to 4 has been adapted from my prior writing, especially my 2017 book "Humanistic Management: Protecting Dignity and Promoting Well-Being," published by Cambridge University.

means but also as an end in themselves. This is not an idealistic vision of people as do-gooders, but is the reason that homo sapiens survived. Moral behavior allows people to build better and longer-lasting relationships that enhance mutual trust and well-being. When they thrive, they are intrinsically motivated to self-actualize and serve others through what they do. Humans do not predictably follow maximization strategies, nor do they have fixed, preconceived utility functions, but their interests, needs, and wants take shape through discourse and a continuous exchange with the outside world. To thrive and be happy, such human beings balance their interests and, in accordance with general moral principles, align them with the interests of others (partners) and their community. Respect for dignity and overall moral behavior are viewed as pathways to well-being and a higher common good.

To summarize, both views of human nature are based on some understanding of human agency and freedom. The economistic perspective highlights *wants* as the foundation of human agency and argues that the maximization of wants is a fundamental human motivation. According to the economistic perspective, fixed utility functions, or opportunity sets centered on their individual benefit above all else, guide humans. The notion of human dignity as a moral cornerstone is absent, and humans are fundamentally considered amoral (not immoral). The highest aspiration for humans is therefore to achieve wealth, power, status, and reputation (see Table 1).

In the humanistic perspective, *evolutionary drives* are the foundational motivation, and achieving a balance is the goal. In the humanistic perspective, humans operate according to routines, yet learn and adapt constantly. According to the humanistic perspective, the key reason for the survival of humans is their relational nature, for which dignity and morality are crucial. Their highest aspiration is to achieve a level of well-being and to flourish.

Table 1 Comparative views on human nature

Human nature	Economistic view	Humanistic view
Foundation	Wants	Drives
Goal	Maximization	Balance
Operating modes	Fixed utility curves/opportunity sets	Routines, learning, practical wisdom
Focal point	Individual	Relational
Role of dignity	Absent	Critical
Role of morality	Amoral	Moral/immoral
Aspiration	Wealth/status/power/reputation	Well-being

The Baseline Model

Evolutionary biology points to four independent drives of human nature, which are critical for the survival of the species. Darwin suggests we share an evolutionary background with many animals, while insights from neuroscience point to deeply rooted neural mechanisms that reward us when we acquire and defend what we deem necessary for survival. Lawrence and Nohria (2002) label two basic drives that we share with all animals as (a) the drive to acquire (dA) and (b) the drive to defend (dD).

The Drive to Acquire (dA)

Lawrence argues that humans, in common with all animals, have a fundamental drive to get what they need to stay alive and have progeny: food, water, warmth, sex, and so on.[115] Modern neuroscience provides evidence to support the biological basis of the drive to acquire. Researchers found, for example, that an area in the brain called the "nucleus accumbens" lights up with increased blood flow when people and animals experience pleasurable sensations from objects they encounter, ranging from tasty food to the sight of a beautiful face. This drive is commonly acknowledged by many economic and management theorists, including Jensen and Meckling, as the basis for utility maximization.

The Drive to Defend (dD)

Lawrence and Nohria claim that in most species the drive to defend is a mirror image of the drive to acquire.[116] What needs defending is what needed to be acquired – food, water, warmth, mates, and so on. Carter and Frith present evidence that the drive to defend seems, like the other drives, to be housed in the limbic area of the brain, specifically in a module called the "amygdala."[117] They explain that the amygdala acts as the brain's alarm system. Depending on the situation, the amygdala will issue a feeling of panic, which translates into a flight mechanism. However, it could also stimulate excessively friendly behavior to appease the opponent. A third response could be to fight, which is increasingly inappropriate in modern civilizations. Lawrence and Nohria further argue that, in humans, the drive to defend means far more – not only the physical necessities of life and procreation but also relationships, cooperative efforts,

---

[115] Lawrence, P. (2010). *Driven to lead: Good, bad, and misguided leadership*. Jossey-Bass.

[116] Lawrence, P., & Nohria, N. (2002). *Driven: How human nature shapes our choices*. Jossey-Bass.

[117] Carter, R., & Frith, C. D. (1998). *Mapping the mind*. University of California Press.

and worldviews (see the idea of protected values).[118] Similar to the drive to acquire, humans can satisfy their drive to defend in a huge variety of ways, and often in cooperation with others.

A Humanistic Extension

Simplified, these two drives (drive to acquire and drive to defend) can explain the economistic perspective on human nature. Within this perspective, all other drives and interests are subordinate to the ambition to maximize the drive to acquire. Spencer's account of Darwin's findings reduced human behavior largely to a two-drive model, which subordinated all other human concerns to the impetus of acquiring and defending.[119]

The novelty of recent evolutionary findings and their importance lie in the addition of two important and *independent* drives, or what Lawrence and Nohria label (1) the drive to bond (dB) and (2) the drive to comprehend (dC).[120] Based on these findings, Paul Lawrence developed a renewed Darwinian theory (RD theory), which rehabilitates Darwin's groundbreaking insights into human behavior, which are often overlooked or misunderstood.[121] In essence, RD theory explains how the human brain has developed via natural selection, as well as through sex and group selection mechanisms, to make complex decisions about all aspects of life (personal, communal, and societal). This theory posits that the two additional drives are independent of the other drives and represent critical ultimate motives that underlie all human decisions: the drive to bond (dB) enables long-term, mutually caring relationships with other humans; and the drive to comprehend (dC) allows us to make sense of the world around us in terms of its multifaceted relations with ourselves. In Darwin's own words:

> The small strength and speed of man, his want of natural weapons, etc., are more than counterbalanced by his *intellectual powers*, through which he has formed himself weapons, tools, etc., and secondly by his *social qualities* which lead him to give and receive aid from his fellow-men.[122]

---

[118] Baron, J., & Spranca, M. (1997). Protected values. *Organizational Behavior and Human Decision Processes, 70*(1), 1–16. Haidt, J. (2012). *The righteous mind: Why good people are divided by politics and religion.* Pantheon.

[119] Lawrence, P. R., & Pirson, M. (2015). Economistic and humanistic narratives of leadership in the age of globality: Toward a renewed Darwinian theory of leadership. *Journal of Business Ethics, 128*(2), 383–394.

[120] Lawrence, P. (2007). Being human – A renewed Darwinian theory of human behavior. www.prlawrence.com. Cambridge, MA. Pirson, M. A., & Lawrence, P. R. (2010). Humanism in business – Towards a paradigm shift? *Journal of Business Ethics, 93*(4), 553–565.

[121] Lawrence, P. (2007). Being human – A renewed Darwinian theory of human behavior. www.prlawrence.com. Cambridge, MA.

[122] Darwin, C. (1909). *The descent of man and selection in relation to sex* (p. 50). Appleton and Company.

In the following section, the evidence for the existence of these two independent drives is presented in more detail. It is important to note that these arguments are still developing, as new evidence is constantly being generated, but the theoretical basis of a four-drive model of human behavior provides propositions that can be tested.

The Drive to Bond (dB)

Aristotle hinted at the drive to bond when he stated that human beings are social animals (*zoon politikon*). Darwin observed the drive to bond in humans when stating:

> Every one will admit that man is a social being. We see this in his dislike of solitude and in his wish for society beyond that of his own family. Solitary confinement is one of the severest punishments which can be inflicted.

or

> Under circumstances of extreme peril, as during a fire, when a man endeavors to save a fellow-creature without a moment's hesitation, he can hardly feel pleasure; and still less has the time to reflect on the dissatisfaction which he might subsequently experience if he did not make the attempt. Should he afterwards reflect over his own conduct, he would feel that there lies within him an impulsive power widely different from a search after pleasure or happiness; and this seems to be the deeply planted social instinct.[123]

These observations seem almost trivial, as most of us will have observed that people tend to form bonds with other people. Lawrence, however, suggests that we need to reevaluate this utterly familiar phenomenon, not simply as "the way people are" or as "the innate goodness in people," but as one of four survival-oriented criteria.[124] Much as E. O. Wilson suggests, the sociality of human nature allowed its survival and the conquest of the Earth.[125]

A number of experiments have offered evidence that there is an independent drive to bond that our brain supports. LeDoux, for example, found that when certain parts of the limbic area – the hypothalamus and anterior thalamus – are impaired, individuals have a difficult time forming

---

[123] Darwin, C. (1909). *The descent of man and selection in relation to sex* (p. 122). Appleton and Company.

[124] Lawrence, P. (2007). Being human – A renewed Darwinian theory of human behavior. www.prlawrence.com. Cambridge, MA.

[125] Wilson, E. O. (2012). *The social conquest of earth*. W. W. Norton & Company.

any meaningful or stable social relationships.[126] Similarly, d'Amasio suggests that damage in certain parts of the brain leaves people lacking emotions, the ability to make rational decisions, and to form new bonds.[127] In experiments that examined group bonding mechanisms, Tajfel found that a group of strangers, divided into arbitrary subgroups, form surprisingly strong attachments to members of the same group, even if the group is completely meaningless and has no prior history.[128] Studies by Warneken and Tomasello, who found that human infants (between 18 and 24 months old) show a spontaneous, unrewarded impulse to help others, even though they seem too young to have learned this behavior from adults, provide further support for the innate and independent drive to bond.[129] In these experiments, researchers, who were strangers to the toddlers, accidentally dropped items and pretended to unsuccessfully reach for them. The children retrieved the items for the experimenter 89 percent of the time. Henrich and colleagues, who find that the value of fairness exists across cultures and trumps the drive to acquire in what is called "the ultimatum game," provide further evidence that this impulse may not be socially learned, but inherent and universal.[130] Searching for homo economicus, the researchers conducted experiments in fifteen countries across the globe to see how people would react when they were offered money, let's say USD 100. This "ultimatum game" allows people to suggest whether and how much they would share their windfall sum. A second person has the right to accept or to reject the offered sum. If the second player rejects it, no one will receive any money. The researchers found that, across the globe, players rarely behaved as homo economicus are expected to behave, that is, either offering or accepting the smallest sum of money. Instead, they largely preferred a "fair" sharing of the cash and rejected "unfair" proposals, even to their detriment. To further highlight how deeply the drive to bond affects us, Lawrence argues that all humans, apart from the

---

[126] LeDoux, J. E. (1996). *The emotional brain: The mysterious underpinnings of emotional life.* Simon & Schuster. LeDoux, J. E. (2002). *Synaptic self: How our brains become who we are.* Viking.

[127] Damasio, A. R. (1994). *Descartes' error: Emotion, reason, and the human brain.* Putnam. Damasio, A. R. (2003). *Looking for Spinoza joy, sorrow, and the feeling brain.* Harcourt.

[128] Tajfel, H. (2010). *Human groups and social categories: Studies in social psychology.* Cambridge University Press.

[129] Warneken, F., & Tomasello, M. (2006). Altruistic helping in human infants and young chimpanzees. *Science, 311*(3), 1301.

[130] Henrich, J., Boyd, R., Bowles, S., Camerer, C., Fehr, E., Gintis, H., & McElreath, R. (2001). In search of homo economicus: Behavioral experiments in 15 small-scale societies. *American Economic Review, 91*(2), 73–78.

rare psychopath, experience pain at the loss of an important long-term relationship, whether by death, divorce, downsizing, or any other causes. For example, emigration is known to cause deep and lasting grief. In many cases, this pain is so deep that a reductionist explanation using the drives to acquire and defend is insufficient.

The Drive to Comprehend (dC)

Aristotle observed the drive to comprehend when he qualified humans as social animals endowed with reason. Many scholars have since suggested that humans have a fundamental drive to understand themselves and their environment. Gribbin and Gribbin refer to it as mankind's insatiable curiosity. Darwin referred to the drive to comprehend by stating:

> As soon as the important faculties of the imagination, wonder, and curiosity, together with some power of reasoning, had become partially developed, man would naturally crave to understand what was passing around him, and could have vaguely speculated on his own existence.[131]

Lawrence argues that the drive to comprehend can be witnessed in the curiosity of children, who ask questions without knowing whether the answers will ever be of any use to them in fulfilling their other drives.[132] Even newborns, once fed and secure, start exploring the world with their eyes and their hands. The popularity of puzzles, Sudoku, or trivia quizzes is also testimony to the independent drive to comprehend, since solving them provides immediate gratification, but only remotely serves other needs. Another supporting argument is that anthropologists have not found a single culture that does not have a creation story, and few that do not have an afterlife story. People seem to need these stories to give meaning to their lives, regardless of whether or not the stories confer any advantage in acquiring, bonding, or defending. Lawrence goes as far as to suggest that religions arose in all societies primarily to help fulfill this drive. Psychologist Steven Pinker argues that the drive to comprehend has helped humans survive against stronger and faster animals by devising weaponry, building houses, and so on.[133] Rather than doing things by instinct, humans tend to figure things out, which in turn can prove very useful as a survival mechanism.

---

[131] Darwin, C. (1909). *The descent of man and selection in relation to sex* (p. 95). Appleton and Company.

[132] Lawrence, P., & Nohria, N. (2002). *Driven: How human nature shapes our choices.* Jossey-Bass.

[133] Pinker, S. (2002). *The blank slate: The modern denial of human nature.* Viking.

Development Toward Independence of Drives

Why is the earlier argument about two different, *independent* drives relevant? After all, bonding and comprehension could simply be used to acquire and defend better, thus supporting the Spencerian, economistic narrative. According to anthropologists and evolutionary psychologists, the independence of the drives to bond and comprehend from the basic drives is key to understanding human evolution. In fact, evolutionary scholars argue that humans have evolved a brain that can continually adapt to its *contemporary* environment, rather than relying on its adaptation to an *ancestral* environment. Accordingly, our brain was an adaptation to a period of extreme and comparatively rapid climatic shifts, the first occurring about two million years ago and the second occurring around 150,000 years ago. These two major shifts explain the development of *independent* drives to bond and to comprehend; the drive to bond emerged when human ancestors transitioned from homo habilis to homo erectus. The drive to comprehend emerged during the shift from homo erectus to homo sapiens.

The Emergence of Bonding

The first evolutionary shift occurred about two million years ago and established the human drive to bond in our neural blueprint. It arguably occurred because pair-bonding proved essential to the survival of the hominid line. Adam Kuper, a South African anthropologist, argues that homo erectus proved fitter for survival than its hominid predecessor, homo habilis, mainly because its brain supported a nuclear family structure.[134] Such a structure proved superior because with increasing brain sizes and slower maturation, offspring needed increased protection. The family bond became a survival mechanism and was probably strengthened by the discovery of fire. Once controlled, fire supported small communities and changed their feeding patterns. Physical anthropologist Richard Wrangham and his colleagues have pointed out that cooking increased the food supply by making it possible to consume plants, such as many roots, that were otherwise toxic or too tough to chew.[135] In addition, cooking

---

[134] Kuper, A. (1994). *The chosen primate: Human nature and cultural diversity.* Harvard University Press.

[135] Wrangham, R. W. (2009). *Catching fire: How cooking made us human.* Basic Books. Wrangham, R. W., Jones, J. H., Laden, G., Pilbeam, D., & Conklin-Brittain, N. (1999). The raw and the stolen: Cooking and the ecology of human origins. *Current Anthropology, 40*(5), 567–594.

helped conserve food and allowed edibles to be stored. The downside of storage was that food would be much more vulnerable to theft, particularly by larger males. According to Wrangham and colleagues, females, who most probably gathered the vegetables, therefore looked for help with guarding the food.[136] Hence, there was a clear evolutionary advantage in mating with a reliable man willing to bond with a particular woman.

There is mounting evidence that the drive to bond is manifested as an independent drive in our brain. The independent status means that the satiation of the drive to bond occurs independently of the satiation of other drives. Nevertheless, research suggests that the brain and the human nervous system reward satiation of the drive to bond in a very similar manner as the drive to acquire and the drive to defend. For example, researchers at the National Institutes of Health scanned the brains of volunteers who had been asked to think about either donating a sum of money to charity or keeping it for themselves.[137] When the volunteers thought about donating the money, a section of the limbic area of their brain lit up. This, surprisingly, was the nucleus accumbens, which usually lights up in response to food or sex. Similar evidence suggests that bonding through, for example, donating money increases human well-being much more than acquiring, such as keeping the money for oneself. Other research suggests that altruism is not necessarily a superior moral faculty for suppressing an egoistic nature, but a hardwired element which leads to pleasure. As such, Lawrence argues that the drive to bond is a full-fledged drive in its own right and is hardwired into the brain.[138]

Comprehension Matters

The shift from homo erectus to homo sapiens finally introduced the drive to comprehend as an independent drive in our neural structure. This shift is known as the Upper Paleolithic Transition (UPT), which is believed to have occurred about 150,000 years ago. According to many evolutionary scholars, homo erectus, who probably only developed very simple tools made of stone and wood, evolved into modern homo sapiens. With this

---

[136] Wrangham, R., Jones, J. H., Laden, G., Pilbeam, D., & Conklin-Brittain, N. (1999). The raw and the stolen: Cooking and the ecology of Human origins. *Current Anthropology*, *40*(5), 567–594.

[137] Zahn, R., Moll, J., Paiva, M., Garrido, G., Krueger, F., Huey, E. D., & Grafman, J. (2009). The neural basis of human social values: Evidence from functional MRI. *Cerebral Cortex*, *19*(2), 276–283.

[138] Lawrence, P. (2007). Being human – A renewed Darwinian theory of human behavior. www.prlawrence.com. Cambridge, MA.

transition, the human species developed language, sophisticated technologies, complex tribal institutions, and civilization as we know it today. Steven Pinker described the dramatic transition in these terms:

> Calling it a revolution is no exaggeration. All other hominids come out of the comic strip *B.C.*, but the Upper Paleolithic people were the Flintstones. More than 45,000 years ago they somehow crossed sixty miles of open ocean to reach Australia, where they left behind hearths, cave paintings, the world's first polished tools, and today's aborigines. Europe (home of the Cro-Magnon) and the Middle East also saw unprecedented arts and technologies, which used new materials like antler, ivory, and bone as well as stone, sometimes transported hundreds of miles. The toolkit included fine blades, needles, awls, many kinds of axes and scrapers, spear points, spear throwers, bows and arrows, fishhooks, engravers, flutes, maybe even calendars. They built shelters, and they slaughtered large animals by the thousands. They decorated everything in sight – tools, cave walls, their bodies – and carved knick-knacks in the shapes of animals and naked women, which archeologists euphemistically call "fertility symbols." They were us... [This] first human revolution was not a cascade of changes set off by a few key inventions. Ingenuity itself was the invention, manifested in hundreds of innovations tens of thousands of miles and years apart.[139]

Pinker's observation that "ingenuity itself was the invention" suggests the emergence of what Lawrence and Nohria call an "independent drive to comprehend" in homo sapiens; increasing empirical evidence points to its independent physical existence in the brain as well.

Neuroscientists Irving Biederman and Edward Vessel found that a part of the brain which helps recognize what we see seems to be equipped with its own reward system of opiate receptors, which give a pleasurable "high" when stimulated by a new image.[140] This pleasurable high can also be experienced when getting a right answer in a trivia quiz or solving a Sudoku. In history, such emotional reactions to "getting it" have also been described as the "Eureka" effect. Increasing evidence demonstrates that humans yearn for novelty, creativity, and understanding because our brain rewards us for it. At the same time, the human brain does not reward routine and monotony, which typically lead to boredom. Biederman and Vessel found that a pleasurable response is diminished when the same image was recognized repeatedly. According to Biederman and Vessel, these opiate receptors get bored by repetition and need new stimulation, which leads us

---

[139] Pinker, S. (1997). *How the mind works* (pp. 202–203). Norton.

[140] Biederman, I., & Vessel, E. (2006). Perceptual pleasure and the brain. *American Scientist*, *94*(3), 247–253.

to curiosity. According to Lawrence, humans are directly rewarded with pleasure when learning something new.[141] The human brain, time and time again, rewards comprehending independently. Throughout evolution, the hardwired reward for learning has had a positive side effect, in that species that learned became more adaptive than species that did not keep learning.

Developing a Humanistic Synthesis – Dignity Matters

In summary, the new humanistic model of human nature builds on insights from the evolutionary sciences. At the base, it posits four basic drives, ultimate motives that underlie all human decisions. There are two ancient drives that all animals with some capacity to sense and evaluate their surroundings share; the drive to acquire (dA) life-sustaining resources, and the drive to defend (dD) against all life-threatening entities. In addition, there are the two newer drives, which evolved to an independent status only in humans: the drive to bond (dB) in order to form long-term mutually caring relationships with other humans, and the drive to comprehend (dC) in order to make sense of the world around us with regard to our own existence.

As can be seen in Figure 1, the economistic model can potentially accommodate these four drives. In contrast, the humanistic view suggests that we have four *independent* underlying natural drives that need to be continually balanced. The humanistic model presupposes that none of the drives can be maximized, but that they need to be in balance to provide a sense of dignity and well-being. In the humanistic model, the independent status of the drives to bond and comprehend means that they are treated as ends in themselves and are rewarded by the brain and nervous system in the same manner as dA or dD. The independence of the four drives thereby renders the model of human nature more complex.

Emerging research in the field of neuroscience finds supportive evidence for the complexity of human drives and suggests that the prefrontal cortex of the brain has been uniquely designed to handle this complexity.[142]

In the humanistic model, the drives to acquire and to defend still remain viable and important factors in determining human behavior, yet the drive to bond with fellow humans and the drive to comprehend are strong, independent, competitive forces. As a result, the four independent drives are

---

[141] Lawrence, P. (2010). *Driven to lead: Good, bad, and misguided leadership*. Jossey-Bass. Biederman, I., & Vessel, E. (2006). Perceptual pleasure and the brain. *American Scientist*, *94*(3), 247–253.

[142] Lawrence, P. R. (2011). What leaders need to know about human evolution and decision making. *Leader to Leader*, 2011(60), 12–16. https://doi.org/10.1002/ltl.462

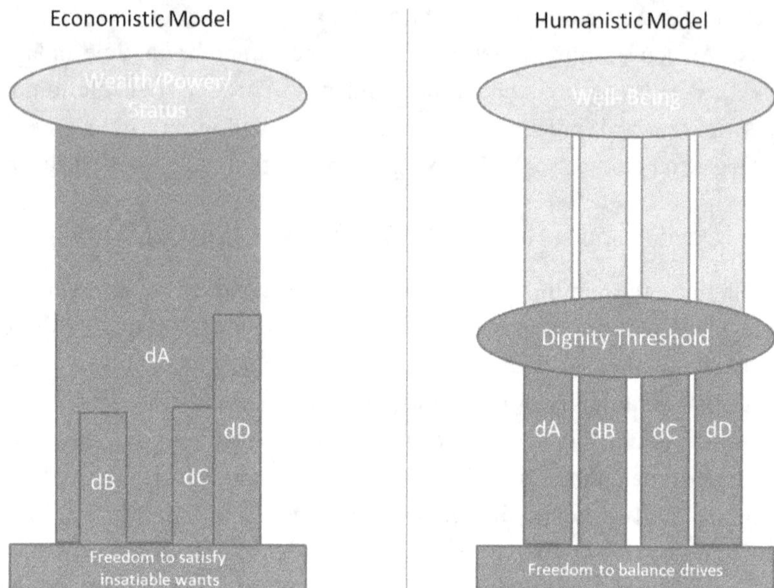

Figure 1 The economistic versus the humanistic model

frequently in conflict with each other. In everyday life, humans struggle to decide how to behave and how to adaptively respond to the immediate circumstances; for example, whether to treat someone with respect or to disregard this person, whether to spend time with children rather than work, or follow the news on Twitter. Lawrence suggests that this condition of drive-conflict brings the prefrontal cortex into action.[143] Its main task is to create a suitable balance when faced with drive-conflict. Neuroscience suggests that the prefrontal cortex has the capacity to call on all the resources of the rest of the cortex (long-term memory, skills, etc.) to search for a response that satisfies all four drives.

EXCURSUS: Psychopathy, Sociopathy, and Humans without Morals

An interesting finding is that REMM actually does seem to have some basis in reality and is not completely unfounded. Whereas most homo sapiens arguably share the ability to be social and have empathy, enabling them to act morally, psychologists argue that there appears to be a minor, but important, exception. Paul Lawrence, for example, argues that across the history of human survival, some people did not develop what he calls the independent drive to bond.[144] These people were asocial and usually

---

[143] Lawrence, P. (2010). *Driven to lead: Good, bad, and misguided leadership*. Jossey-Bass.
[144] Ibid.

outcasts in society. Throughout evolution, they had been marginalized, but never completely eradicated because they coexisted as parasites. In fact, it is estimated that about 1 percent of the population lacks an independent drive to bond, causing what is otherwise known as "psychopathy."[145] Psychologist Robert Hare, a leading researcher on psychopathy for more than thirty years, describes psychopaths as:

> ...social predators who charm, manipulate, and ruthlessly plow their way through life, leaving a broad trail of broken hearts, shattered expectations, and empty wallets. Completely lacking in conscience and in feelings for others, they selfishly take what they want and do as they please, violating social norms and expectations without the slightest sense of guilt or regret.[146]

They have "an insatiable appetite for power and control,"[147] combined with "a deeply disturbing inability to care about the pain and suffering experienced by others – in short, a complete lack of empathy."[148] Researchers have identified psychopaths (whom biologists and economists call "free-riders" and whom sociologists and some psychologists tend to call "sociopaths") as people with a genetic defect.[149] They are incapable of empathy and have no skill set of conscience or morality. Their jaw-dropping selfishness and lack of empathy do not come from exaggerated drives to acquire and defend; these drives are normal – which means they are innate, unconscious, independent, and insatiable – but are not checked and balanced by a drive to have trusting and caring relationships with others.[150] Lawrence describes them as wild animals – motivated mainly by

---

[145] Hare, R. D. (1999). *Without conscience: The disturbing world of the psychopaths among us*. Guilford Press. Neumann, C. S., & Hare, R. D. (2008). Psychopathic traits in a large community sample: Links to violence, alcohol use, and intelligence. *Journal of Consulting and Clinical Psychology*, *76*(5), 893–899.

[146] Hare, R. D. (1999). *Without conscience: The disturbing world of the psychopaths among us* (p. XI). Guilford Press.

[147] Hare, R. D. (1999). *Without conscience: The disturbing world of the psychopaths among us* (p. 281). Guilford Press.

[148] Hare, R. D. (1999). *Without conscience: The disturbing world of the psychopaths among us* (p. 6). Guilford Press.

[149] Neumann, C. S., & Hare, R. D. (2008). Psychopathic traits in a large community sample: Links to violence, alcohol use, and intelligence. *Journal of Consulting and Clinical Psychology*, *76*(5), 893–899. Weber, S., Habel, U., Amuts, K., & Schneider, F. (2008). Structural brain abnormalities in psychopaths: A review. *Behavioral Sciences & the Law*, *26*(7), 7–28.

[150] Buckholtz, J. W., Treadway, M. T., Cowan, R. L., Woodward, N. D., Benning, S. D., Li, R., Ansari, M. S., Baldwin, R. M., Schwartzman, A. N., Shelby, E. S., Smith, C. E., Cole, D., Kessler, R. M., & Zald, D. H. (2010). Mesolimbic dopamine reward system hypersensitivity in individuals with psychopathic traits. *Nature Neuroscience*, *13*(4), 419–421.

the two universal animal drives – but with all the advantages of a human drive to comprehend.[151]

Hare estimates – conservatively, he insists – that "there are at least 2 million psychopaths in North America; the citizens of New York City have as many as 100,000 psychopaths among them."[152] Hare and Babiak even argue that many of these psychopaths gain influence and power and that the current corporate environment allows them to do so effectively.[153] In fact, recent research indicates that psychopaths are overrepresented in current business institutions, including Wall Street; estimates range from 6 percent to 10 percent psychopaths in leadership functions.[154] Historians have made the argument that, across history, many examples of bad leadership can be traced to psychopathic personalities, including Hitler, Stalin, and even Napoleon.[155]

Conclusion

Taking the four-drive model as its basis, the leadership and managerial task every human naturally undertakes is to balance rather than maximize any of the four drives. If we try to maximize any of the drives – at the individual, group, or societal level – we risk distress, conflict, and ultimately extinction, as we will see in the next section.

5 Balancing Not Maximizing

The **Goldilocks principle** is named by analogy to the children's story "The Three Bears," in which a young girl named Goldilocks tastes three different bowls of porridge and finds she prefers porridge that is neither too hot nor too cold but has just the right temperature. The concept of "just the right amount" is easily understood and applied to a wide range of disciplines, including developmental psychology, biology, astronomy, economics, and engineering.[156]

---

[151] Lawrence, P. (2010). *Driven to lead: Good, bad, and misguided leadership*. Jossey-Bass.

[152] Hare, R. D. (1999). *Without conscience: The disturbing world of the psychopaths among us* (pp. 1–2). Guilford Press.

[153] Babiak, P., & Hare, R. D. (2006). *Snakes in suits: When psychopaths go to work*. Regan Books.

[154] Babiak, P., & Hare, R. D. (2006). *Snakes in suits: When psychopaths go to work*. Regan Books. Lawrence, P. (2010). *Driven to lead: Good, bad, and misguided leadership*. Jossey-Bass. Boddy, C. R. (2011). The corporate psychopaths theory of the global financial crisis. *Journal of Business Ethics, 102*(2), 255–259.

[155] Neumayr, A. (1995). *Dictators in the mirror of medicine: Napoleon, Hitler, Stalin*. Medi-Ed Press.

[156] https://en.wikipedia.org/wiki/Goldilocks_principle (accessed January 23, 2025).

We all know that there can be too much or too little of something, that it can be too cold or too hot. Aristotle called the ideal state the "golden mean." Goldilocks settled for just the right temperature and many spiritual leaders similarly remind us to adhere to temperance, prudence, and mindfulness. Kate Raworth calls the societal zone that represents the golden mean the safe and just zone for humanity.[157] In this zone, the four basic drives are balanced and satisfied at a level that allows people to feel human. Donna Hicks calls that state "dignity."[158] I argue that good management and leadership support all stakeholders to move beyond the dignity level and stay within the planetary boundaries. Buckminster Fuller called this state a world that works for 100 percent of humanity.[159]

Balancing the Four Drives: Key to Survival, Longevity, and Happiness

As managers and leaders, and simply as those who wish to survive and thrive, we are able to balance the four drives. Not only Goldilocks but also Aristotle and the Dalai Lama remind us that such an act of mindfulness is the key to a good life. This balancing act is also evident in those who are considered the happiest people.

In a much-cited and criticized study on blue zones, places in the world that have many more centenarians than others, author Daniel Buettner discovered a balance of the four drives.[160] Buettner started by asking himself why life expectancy and happiness have been declining in the most prosperous nation in history, the United States. He started to study the question: if prosperity isn't improving our well-being, what else could?

In a well-known documentary, he outlined the results of his twenty-year-long research into the lifestyle habits of the world's healthiest, longest-lived individuals.[161] Among other things, these include:

- Move naturally: rather than engaging in intense exercise, long-lived individuals live in environments that naturally encourage movement, such as gardening and performing manual tasks without relying on machines.

---

[157] Raworth, K. & Oxfam. (2012). A safe and just space for humanity: Can we live within the doughnut? In *Oxfam Discussion Papers*. www-cdn.oxfam.org/s3fs-public/file_attachments/dp-a-safe-and-just-space-for-humanity-130212-en_5.pdf

[158] Hicks, D. (2013). *Dignity: Its essential role in resolving conflict.* Yale University Press.

[159] Fuller, R. B. (2008). *Utopia or oblivion: The prospects for humanity.* Lars Müller Publishers.

[160] Buettner, D., & Skemp, S. (2016). Blue zones. *American Journal of Lifestyle Medicine, 10*(5), 318–321. https://doi.org/10.1177/1559827616637066

[161] Ibid.

- 80% rule: following the Okinawan mantra "hara hachi bu," they stop eating when 80% full, leading to better weight management.
- Plant slant: their diets emphasize beans and limit meat consumption to around five times per month, with small portion sizes.
- Wine @ 5: Moderate alcohol consumption, preferably wine, is common among long-lived individuals and is enjoyed in moderation with meals and friends.

Hence, to fulfil the drive to acquire, people in the blue zones move naturally, eat moderately, and even drink some wine.

In a way, these results[162] confirm the evidence from evolutionary biology and suggest that a long life can be had by balancing the four drives, not by maximizing one of them.

To fulfil the drive to bond, the communities strongly emphasize love and belonging:

- Belong: being part of a faith-based community is common among centenarians and is associated with increased life expectancy.
- Loved ones first: prioritizing family, keeping aging relatives nearby, and investing time and love in relationships contribute to longevity.
- Right tribe: long-lived individuals surround themselves with supportive social circles that encourage healthy behaviors.

To address the drive to comprehend, they nurture a sense of purpose that goes beyond belonging or acquisition.

- Purpose: having a sense of purpose, referred to as "Ikigai" in Okinawa and "plan de vida" in Nicoya, can add up to seven years to life expectancy.

To address the drive to defend, they manage stress and create safe spaces for themselves:

- Downshift: long-lived individuals have routines to manage stress, such as reflecting on ancestors, praying, taking naps, or socializing.

While researchers have questioned the original data that predicted longevity in blue zones, studies have found that applying the principles can nevertheless improve longevity and well-being.[163] Adopting such practices

---

[162] Ibid.

[163] Holt-Lunstad, J., Smith, T. B., & Layton, J. B. (2010). *Social relationships and mortality risk*. PLOS Medicine. Black, D. S., & Slavich, G. M. (2016). *Mindfulness meditation and the immune system*. Annals of the New York Academy of Sciences.

in places outside the original blue zones, researchers found that putting in place routines that support the balance of the four drives can increase life expectancy and quality of life in a rather predictable manner.[164] Buettner and his critics argue that, while genetics play a role in longevity, adopting a blue zones lifestyle can significantly increase life expectancy and improve overall health.[165] The current research on longevity and happiness concurs that a balance of the four drives is at the source of better living.[166]

When More Kills

When we talk about leadership and management, in many cases people fall into the trap of maximization. In recent times, it has become popular to talk about purpose maximization, or the maximization of psychological safety, or maximizing trust. All of these are maximization strategies that ultimately hurt us. The impacts of our maximization strategies are hidden in plain sight. In the following section, I provide some occasionally brutal evidence of our species' attempts to minimize or maximize any of the four drives, which ultimately lead to death and extinction.

Overdosing on the Drive to Acquire

Moritz Erhardt, 21, was found dead in his shower after working 72 hours straight. Erhardt was an ambitious finance student from Southwest Germany interning for Bank of America Merrill Lynch. He had performed well in the banking industry, which involved working extremely long hours, and as a result was about to land a much-coveted investment banking job in the city of London. As one of his colleagues shared at the time of Erhardt's death, working for more than 100 hours was normal, but he said that despite the pressures, he and other interns enjoyed the experience.[167]

However, persistent sleep deprivation and chronic stress have deadly consequences. Jeffrey Pfeffer's research highlights that work-related stress

---

[164] Kreouzi, M., Theodorakis, N., & Constantinou, C. (2024) Lessons learned from blue zones, lifestyle medicine pillars and beyond: An update on the Contributions of behavior and genetics to wellbeing and longevity. *American Journal of Lifestyle Medicine, 18*(6), 750–765. https://doi.org/10.1177/15598276221118494

[165] Malm, E. K., Roberson, L. B., Dada, O., Naber, J. L., Dodd, A., Thurmond, J., & Heinrich, E. (2024). Sense of purpose, reduced stress, and connection as protective factors for longevity: An exploration of barriers. *American Journal of Health Education, 55*, 1–13. https://doi.org/10.1080/19325037.2024.2366465

[166] Seligman, M. (2018). PERMA and the building blocks of well-being. *The Journal of Positive Psychology, 13*(4), 333–335.

[167] Malik, S. (2017, December 1). Moritz Erhardt intern death spurs Bank of America Merrill Lynch review. *The Guardian.* www.theguardian.com/business/2013/aug/23/intern-death-bank-of-america-merrill-lynch

alone contributes to 120,000 premature deaths annually in the United States.[168] CEO Bob Chapman of Barry-Wehmiller even attributes the health crisis to CEOs themselves. This aligns with data showing that a significant portion of healthcare costs in developed countries, particularly in the United States, stem from chronic diseases such as diabetes, cardiovascular diseases, and metabolic syndromes, exacerbated by stress-related behaviors like substance abuse, overeating, and lack of exercise. Numerous studies indicate that the workplace is a primary source of stress. Yale and the Families and Work Institute have found that approximately three in five Americans frequently experience burnout or high levels of stress in their jobs.[169]

When More Is Not Better

Keith Martin was a bed-bound Londoner. He died aged 44, weighing almost 1,000 lbs. According to the British press, he consumed on average 20,000 calories a day in a diet that included six-egg fried breakfasts and lunches and dinners consisting of pizzas, kebabs, take-outs, and Big Macs. He washed this down with 3.5 liters of coffee and two liters of fizzy drinks. Matthew Crawford hit the headlines when he cost the National Health Service hundreds of thousands of British pounds by blocking four hospital beds for over eighteen months. He had to be treated when hitting more than 700 pounds (300 kg). He died prematurely at the age of 37.

When More Is Not Better – 2

Mary was a small-town girl, one of fifteen kids born into a rather well-to-do family. Historians report she learned to love fashion and the power clothing could provide. Mary met Abraham and Abe was up to big things. He became president of the United States, one many consider the finest. Yet his wife had developed an obsession with shopping. "She was considered addicted to shopping, running up (and concealing) large bills on credit, feeling manic glee at spending sprees, followed by depressive reactions in the face of the results."[170]

---

[168] Pfeffer, J. (2018). *Dying for a paycheck: How modern management harms employee Health and Company performance – and what we can ao about it.* HarperBusiness.

[169] Abramson, A. (n.d.). *Burnout and stress are everywhere.* www.apa.org. www.apa.org/monitor/2022/01/special-burnout-stress

[170] Hague, B., Hall, J., & Kellett, S. (2016). Treatments for compulsive buying: A systematic review of the quality, effectiveness and progression of the outcome evidence. *Journal of Behavioral Addictions, 5*(3), 379–394.

Compulsive buying disorder and diseases of affluence are labelled "Western diseases" that have developed with increasing wealth in a society. They are in contrast to so-called diseases of poverty.

The previous examples are extreme and show that there are limits to growth and the negative impact of wanting more. Yet we often live life with the unconscious or subconscious assumption that more is better. While intuitively we all know better, the example of Ethan Couch shows that too much is deadly. Ethan Couch was sixteen when he killed four people while driving while drunk. At his manslaughter trial, the psychologist told the juvenile court that he was affected by affluenza or irresponsibility caused by family wealth. Arguably, too much wealth caused the death of four innocent bystanders. So, not only is too much acquisition bad for self, it is bad for others.

Overdosing on the Drive to Bond

Throughout the course of human history, human beings have put the in-group above the out-group and oftentimes above the self – with significant costs. To highlight an example that seems all too common, here is an excerpt from the *New York Post* from July 13, 2021:

> Jaryan Eliot, a 13-year-old gangbanger <u>was shot dead</u> amid a raging Bronx street war. Two weeks before he had shared with his pals that he wanted to leave the gang called Crips. His grief-stricken pals told The NY Post: "Two weeks ago we was with him, and he was telling us how he was tired of this gang stuff. He wanted to get some money and get out of the' hood," said a 16-year-old female friend of Jaryan Elliot, the Crips member who was fatally shot Sunday in revenge for a gang slaying four days earlier.
>
> Jaryan's pal lamented that gangs are so revered in the area that her little brother boasts he's in one, even though he's not. "He is only 10 years old. He is saying that he is in a gang," she said. "He thinks it's cute, but I tell him he is not in no gang. He is only 10 years old." Jaryan's former girlfriend said she tried to warn him about being in a gang.
>
> "He was the youngest of all of them. July 29th, he would be 14," she said of her doomed gang-member ex, who had only just graduated middle school.[171]

---

[171] Roberts, G., & Sheehy, K. (2021, July 13). Exclusive | Teen gang member fatally shot in the Bronx was trying to leave Crips, pal says. *New York Post.* https://nypost.com/2021/07/13/teen-gang-member-fatally-shot-in-the-bronx-was-trying-to-leave-crips-pal/

Overdosing on Bonding as a Society

Overdosing on bonding has consistently shown up as tribalism, nationalism, and racism and has caused many wars and left millions dead – the obvious opposite of survival. To highlight the extreme bonding of an ingroup versus an out-group, the diaries of Anne Frank are used to educate and warn. Further is an account of how Anne Frank's family was arrested and then brought to Bergen Belsen, a Nazi concentration camp.

> To the people in hiding, it was the 761th day in the Secret Annex, more than two years since the day Anne and her family had entered the hiding place on 6 July 1942. Between half past ten and eleven in the morning, police officers showed up at the building at Prinsengracht 263. *SS Hauptscharführer* Karl Silberbauer was in charge. The people in hiding were completely taken by surprise. For more than two years they had been living with the constant fear of discovery. And now, without any warning, the moment had come. Otto: "I was upstairs with the Van Pels family in Peter's room, helping him with his schoolwork. Suddenly someone came running up the stairs and then the door opened and there was a man right in front of us with a pistol in his hand. Downstairs they were all gathered. My wife, the children, and the Van Pels family all stood there with their hands up in the air."[172]
>
> Fritz Pfeffer was also taken into the room. The people in hiding had to hand in their valuables. Silberbauer took Otto's briefcase, which contained Anne's diary papers, and emptied it out to put the valuables in. Anne's diary papers fell to the wooden floor. The group had to prepare for departure. Helpers Victor Kugler and Johannes Kleiman were arrested together with the eight people from the Secret Annex. The police officers took them away. By then, it was around 1 pm: the raid had taken a little over two hours.[173]

Anne Frank, whose diary was found and published posthumously, and her family were deported to Bergen Belsen concentration camp and died in February 1945, three months before liberation.

Overdosing on the Drive to Comprehend

In a similarly horrific fashion, the maximization of the drive to comprehend kills. We have all heard about jihadists or crusaders, people willing

---

[172] Broek, G. (2016). August 4, 1944 Dr. Gertjan Broek Anne Frank House. www.annefrank.org/en/downloads/filer_public/38/bc/38bc0487-5ba4-4668-a47e-0ea1d7a00766/eng_artikel_arrestatie.pdf (accessed March 4, 2024); Schnabel, E. (1958). Anne Frank: Spur eines Kindes.

[173] Ibid.

to die for their convictions and purpose. In many cases they are celebrated by their peer group and are often revered over the years as martyrs for the cause.[174]

Take the example of Dita Oepriarto and Puji Kuswanti, who took their children and blew themselves up, killing twelve people and injuring more than forty others severely.[175]

> According to the news reports Dita Oepriarto, the father, drove a van to the Indonesian Christian Church and dropped off his wife Puji Kuswat and their 9- and 12-year-old daughters. According to the news reports the wife and daughters went inside and detonated a bomb. The father then drove the van to the Pentecost Central Church, where, from inside the vehicle, he detonated another bomb in front of the church. At the same time, Oepriarto's sons drove motorcycles to Santa Maria Catholic Church, where they, too, detonated bombs. According to CCTV footage, the bomb at that church went off at 7:08 a.m. Forensic evidence indicates the bombs were attached to the attackers' bodies.[176]

> Dita and Puji were devoted parents and more devoted to their version of faith that encouraged them to kill people of other faiths and becoming martyrs. Friends from earlier in their lives said: I wasn't actually too surprised when he finally blew himself up with his family as the culmination of his 'jihad,' because the seeds of extremism have been planted since 30 years ago.[177]

When notified of the killings, Pope Francis prayed for the victims of the attacks during his weekly Sunday address. The pope, a peaceful man, is successor to many other faith-inspired massacres such as the crusades. To remind some of the atrocities committed by faith maximizers, here an account (Figure 2):

> In July 1099, European armies, fresh from the siege of Antioch, converged on Jerusalem (then ruled by the Muslim Fatimid Dynasty) and attacked the walled city from two sides. On the north, the crusaders would eventually breach the walls and perpetrate a slaughter that still echoes across the centuries. But on the south, a deep, wide ditch just outside the city's wall kept the siege towers from approaching to disgorge their cargoes of armed men. A priest traveling with the army of

---

[174] Juergensmeyer, M. (2017b). *Terror in the mind of god, fourth edition: The global rise of religious violence.* University of California Press.

[175] Family of suicide bombers attacks 3 churches in Indonesia, killing 12, police say | CNN (accessed March 5, 2024).

[176] Ibid.

[177] www.nytimes.com/2018/05/27/insider/indonesian-family-suicide-bombers.html (accessed January 23, 2025).

Figure 2 Maximizing the drive to comprehend has often
been a cause for war

Raymond de Saint Gilles, the Count of Toulouse, described the ditch
and the crusaders' efforts to advance. Toulouse reportedly offered
his troops an extra payment of gold dinars to venture close to the
guarded walls under cover of darkness and fill in part of the ditch. The
Frenchmen succeeded; their siege tower got through, slamming against
the stone wall of Jerusalem to bring them face to face with an enemy
who had traded arrow volleys with them for the last five weeks.

Despite that small victory, the southern assault on Jerusalem failed.
Even with a few siege towers in place, the southern wall was too well-
defended to breach. Although Jerusalem's southern defenses held, the
invaders ultimately overran the city. And when they did, there was nothing noble or holy in their conquest.

"The chroniclers talk about 'rivers of blood' running in the streets of
the city, and it may not be an exaggeration," said Shimon Gibson, a
historian at the University of North Carolina at Charlotte. Amid loot-
ing, burning, and worse, crusaders slaughtered Muslims, Jews, and
even local Christians, whom they considered heretics. "They turned
Jerusalem into a ghost town," said Gibson.[178]

Overdosing on the Drive to Defend

Ted Kaczynski was described as a brilliant student. He entered Harvard
in 1958 at the age of fifteen and reportedly wrote one of the best doctoral
dissertations in mathematics at the University of Michigan. However,

---

[178] Smith, K. (2019, July 25). *Archeologists confirm near-legendary tale of crusaders' siege
of Jerusalem | The Shelby White and Leon Levy.* https://whitelevy.fas.harvard.edu/news/
archeologists-confirm-near-legendary-tale-crusaders%E2%80%99-siege-jerusalem

he resigned his professorial post at UC Berkeley to withdraw and live in the woods of Montana. There he developed a perspective on the world that fueled his hatred of technological society and the damage done to the environment. He started a nationwide campaign against those he believed to be promoting modern technology and environmental degradation. He killed three people and left twenty-three severely injured by sending bombs via US postal mail. In 1996, he was identified as the "Unabomber." He was sentenced to eight life sentences without chances of parole, merely escaping the death penalty.

From gun addicts to doomsday sect adherents to the "castle societies" of Europe in the Middle Ages, when defense becomes the primary objective of life, life itself can easily become short.

It may seem intuitive that moderation and prudence are key to a long life. It could be blindingly obvious that too little of that which sustains life can kill. Still, this is a revolutionary insight for business leadership and management as well as economics and politics. In many ways, the intellectual paradigm underlying global economics and politics has endorsed maximization strategies.[179]

Poverty (of Dignity) Kills

Tom Friedman, the renowned *New York Times* columnist, suggests that there is a poverty of dignity rather than a poverty of money. This poverty of dignity is arguably fueling massive global conflicts. It also is the source of widening political divides and a drift toward extremes. Through the lens of the four-drive theory, we can see what that may mean when basic human drives remain under-fulfilled.

Underdosing the Drive to Acquire

It's widely recognized that inadequate access to food or living in poverty can significantly diminish one's quality of life. As Robert Sapolsky from Stanford University emphasizes, poverty, as the most pervasive form of social subordination in humans, contributes to poor health through various mechanisms.[180] What might be less apparent is that not only material

---

[179] Sen, A. (1997). Maximization and the act of choice. *Econometrica: Journal of the Econometric Society, 65*(4), 745–779. Sachs, J. (2008). *Common wealth: Economics for a crowded planet.* Penguin. Simmons, B. A., & Elkins, Z. (2004). The globalization of liberalization: Policy diffusion in the international political economy. *American Political Science Review, 98*(1), 171–189.

[180] Sapolsky, R. M. (2005). The influence of social hierarchy on primate health. *Science, 308*(5722), 648–652. https://doi.org/10.1126/science.1106477

deprivation but also low social status can shorten lifespan. Decades of research suggest that higher social status positively impacts health, while chronic stress resulting from low social status can be detrimental, especially when experienced early in life. Robert Sapolsky, a prominent stress researcher who has extensively studied baboons, notes that human societies have created dominance hierarchies unlike anything seen in the primate world, with those at the bottom facing particularly adverse health outcomes.[181] Indeed, studies demonstrate that individuals with lower socioeconomic status tend to have shorter lifespans and higher rates of disease compared to their wealthier counterparts, even after accounting for factors like access to healthcare.[182]

However, there exists a solution for alleviating stress related to social status, even within contexts of social inequality. Although humans don't engage in grooming behaviors like baboons, studies indicate that strong social support, particularly through physical contact such as hugs and massages, can effectively reduce the impact of stress in humans as well. While not everyone can occupy alpha or beta positions, we all have the capacity to give and receive love, according to *Maia Szalavitz, a health writer for* TIME.com.[183]

For Jenny Tung, a professor of evolutionary anthropology, all hope is not lost: "We've convincingly shown that chronic social stress by itself can change the way our body works," she says, "But the hopeful message is how responsive [immune] systems are to changes in the social environment. That's really different than the possibility that your social history stays with you your entire life."[184]

Underdosing the Drive to Bond

Another way we can violate dignity is by exclusion. The rise in Diversity, Equity, and Inclusion (DEI) initiatives can be viewed as a process of reclaiming dignity. At its core, social exclusion and isolation are some of the most powerful punishments humans have come up with. They mess

---

[181] Ibid.

[182] Ibid.

[183] Szalavitz, M. (2012, May 22). *Baboon study shows why high social status boosts health | TIME.com.* TIME.com. https://healthland.time.com/2012/05/22/baboon-study-shows-why-high-social-status-boosts-health/#:~:text=There%20is%2C%20however%2C%20a%20remedy,of%20stress%20for%20humans%2C%20too

[184] Caruso, C. (2024, February 20). Who's top monkey? How social status affects immune health. *Scientific American.* www.scientificamerican.com/article/whos-top-monkey-how-social-status-affects-immune-health/#:~:text=For%20Tung%2C%20however%2C%20the%20outlook,changes%20in%20the%20social%20environment

with the social nature of humans and impact the brain in such a way that many people "go crazy" or commit suicide.

To illustrate the detrimental effects of social isolation leading individuals to self-harm, inmates in Texas initiated a hunger strike. Confined in solitary units, Texas prisoners observed fellow inmates deteriorate mentally, some tragically resorting to suicide. With thousands enduring prolonged periods of extreme isolation for years or even decades, a cohort of individuals resolved in 2023 to raise awareness about their plight. By January 10, approximately 300 men in prisons across the state had joined in a hunger strike to protest against Texas' solitary confinement policies. They claimed their dignity by stating "We are humans back here."[185]

In contrast, anthropologists report that indigenous societies practice a social inclusion approach to offenders by reminding them of their higher selves and integrating them even more closely into society. There may be a good reason Robinson Crusoe was fictional.

Underdosing the Drive to Comprehend

In 2018, the Centers for Disease Control and Prevention published startling data regarding the surge in suicide deaths in the United States, showing a 25-percent increase since 1999 across various ethnicities and age-groups.[186] These figures unequivocally indicate a crisis, but what kind of crisis exactly? Many argue that this reflects a crisis in mental healthcare, suggesting that individuals are not receiving the necessary services. The proposed solution involves improving therapies, developing more effective antidepressants, and enhancing access to treatment. While this assessment may be valid, the suicide rate has continued to rise despite more people seeking treatment for depression and anxiety and despite the increased availability of treatments for these conditions.

Therefore, an additional explanation appears necessary. Behavioral scientists specializing in fundamental psychological needs, such as the need for meaning, assert that the suicide crisis partly stems from a sense of meaninglessness. Addressing this crisis comprehensively requires an understanding of how recent societal changes – toward increased detachment and weakened social bonds – are heightening the risk of existential despair.

---

[185] McCullough, J. (2024, February 6). After 21 days, final Texas prisoner ends hunger strike against solitary confinement. *The Texas Tribune.* www.texastribune.org/2023/01/30/texas-prisons-hunger-strike-letters/

[186] Suicide Data and Statistics. (2024, October 29). Suicide Prevention. www.cdc.gov/suicide/facts/data.html#:~:text=Suicide%20rates%20increased%2037%25%20between,to%20their%20peak%20in%202022

Empirical studies bear this out. A felt lack of meaning in one's life has been linked to alcohol and drug abuse, depression, anxiety and – yes – suicide. And when people experience loss, stress, or trauma, it is those who believe that their lives have a purpose who are best able to cope with and recover from distress.

Underdosing the Drive to Defend

It seems painfully obvious: if people don't feel safe either physically or psychologically, they will not survive or thrive. Ask anyone who has experienced conditions of war or abuse. Still, physical and emotional violence are a standard experience across the globe. While in some areas physical safety seems more common (at least in most Western workplace settings), the importance of psychological safety is becoming more central.

A study conducted in 2017 showcases that psychological safety in many workplaces is alarmingly low.[187] Dr. Meisha-Ann Martin, director of people analytics at Workhuman, argues that only 26 percent of workers felt psychologically secure during the pandemic, experiencing heightened levels of burnout, stress, and increased feelings of isolation.

Psychological safety encompasses the ability to express oneself authentically at work, take risks, and be vulnerable without fear of negative repercussions. However, when individuals are experiencing burnout, stress, and loneliness, it becomes challenging for them to bring their full selves to work. The findings from Workhuman's study indicate:

- 48% of respondents somewhat or strongly agreed that they have experienced burnout.
- 61% have reported elevated stress levels.
- 32% somewhat or strongly agreed that they have felt lonely while at work.

The absence of psychological safety in the workplace can lead to numerous issues, including decreased productivity and a lack of genuine work relationships. However, the alarming reality is that the absence of psychological safety can result in severe, even fatal, consequences. One illustrative case is Boeing, where employees feared reprisals if they raised concerns about the 737 Max models. This fear ultimately contributed to two plane

---

[187] Newman, A., Donohue, R., & Eva, N. (2017). Psychological safety: A systematic review of the literature. *Human Resource Management Review*, *27*(3), 521–535. https://doi.org/10.1016/j.hrmr.2017.01.001

crashes that claimed hundreds of lives. Had these Boeing employees felt empowered to voice their concerns, these tragic incidents might have been prevented.[188]

Balancing, Not Maximizing, Any of the Four Drives

Aristotle described human beings as *social animals endowed with reason.* In my conversations with Paul Lawrence, he said that all evolutionary evidence points to the same conclusion. *Social* represents the drive to bond, *animals* highlights the basic drives to acquire and defend we share with all living beings, and *endowed with reason* corresponds with the drive to comprehend that sets us apart as homo sapiens. Aristotle was also the inspiration for many scholars of human happiness and human well-being. It is not a surprise, then, that much of the evidence gathered has come to similar conclusions regarding human happiness. The happiest human beings apparently are able to balance the satisfaction of their four basic and independent drives.

One of the leading figures in the study of human well-being, Martin Seligman, created a model that confirms the independence of connected components of human well-being that consists of positivity, engagement, relationships, meaning, and accomplishments (PERMA). Relationships arguably fit the drive to bond, meaning refers to the drive to comprehend and accomplishments the drive to acquire. Positivity and engagement are only possible when safety is present.

Conclusion

As such, Goldilocks had it right. If we as humans want to survive, thrive, and live a long life, we should avoid maximization strategies. We clearly have fundamental dignity requirements to feel alive as well and those are often considered our social minima or basic human needs. These basic needs do include financial and material wealth but are not fulfilled by them. In many ways, merely wealthy people are not able to find their humanity until they feel safe, cared for, and serve a higher purpose. While this insight might strike some as trivial and obvious, the balancing objective has deep-rooted and radical consequences for our lives and those of others.

---

[188] Robinson, B. (2021, June 15). 10 red flags that psychological safety is lacking in your workplace. *Forbes.* www.forbes.com/sites/bryanrobinson/2021/06/13/10-red-flags-that-psychological-safety-is-lacking-in-your-workplace/?sh=6886364110c1

6 Humanistic Management in Practice

We all engage with those around us using an implicit blueprint of human beings. For managers, the critical stepping stone for success is an accurate understanding of the stakeholders they work with. There have always been business leaders that intuitively understood human beings better than others. This better understanding serves as the source of their superior market performance. Unfortunately, in business education we systematically distort our intuition and supplant it with the homo economicus approach. Furthermore, our general culture embraces the homo economicus assumptions to society's detriment. The tragedy is that we are not seeing it.

The humanistic model of human nature is not only more accurate and realistic, but it also explains our own longevity, survival, and happiness and is highly relevant when we want to address some of the major global crises humanity faces. For example, if we stopped seeing people as narrowly egoistic and self-serving, we could see humans as truly interested in their well-being and that of others. We would then be open to a strong yearning for organizations that pursue a higher purpose, such as social enterprises, B-corporations, conscious businesses, and the economy for the common good. It should be no surprise, then, that Larry Fink, the CEO of BlackRock, considers it an investment risk if CEOs of public corporations don't build trust with their stakeholders and serve a societal purpose. Yet, the pushback against such ideas is massive.[189]

In his book *Driven to Lead: Good, Bad, and Misguided Leadership* (2010), Paul Lawrence writes that good leaders intuitively know that they have to balance the four drives within themselves, with others, and within society (see Figure 3).[190] Lawrence compares organizations to cars with four-cylinder engines. Good organizations, according to Lawrence, run on all four cylinders rather than one. These organizations are able to create a purpose beyond profit (dC) and are able to establish good relationships based on trust with the various stakeholders with whom they collaborate (dB). Lawrence suggests that bad and misguided organizational leaders try to focus on only one or two drives, say profit maximization (dA) and competitiveness (dD).

According to Lawrence, bad leadership follows a psychopathic model of human behavior and solely wishes to fulfill the drive to acquire. These leaders wish to achieve status, rank, and profit more than anything. They

<hr>

[189] www.knowesg.com/featured-article/the-anti-esg-movement-explained (accessed January 23, 2025).

[190] Lawrence, P. R. (2010). *Driven to lead: Good, bad, and misguided leadership.* Jossey-Bass, Cop.

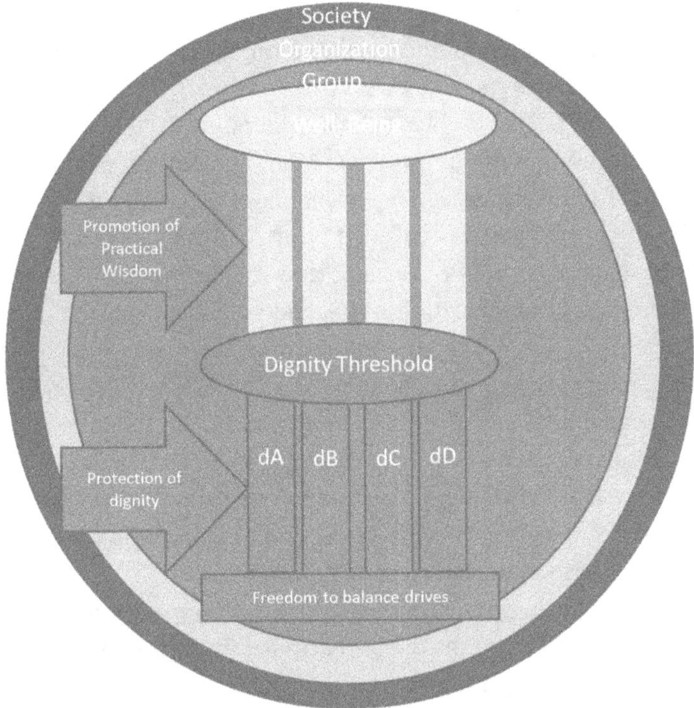

Figure 3 Humanistic perspectives on leadership

Source: Author

sometimes acknowledge the other drives, but mainly to enhance the drive to acquire. The bestselling management author Jim Collins, for example, highlights the example of the US corporate executive Albert J. Dunlap, who went into organizations to slash costs in the short term and hike up shareholder value, only to leave after a very short stint at the helm, taking several hundreds of millions of dollars as compensation with him. The business press is replete with examples of leaders that ignore the dignity of their employees to gain power.

Misguided leadership can be understood as that which follows an economistic perspective. Leaders may very well sense, for example, that they cannot motivate employees by focusing on profit maximization; nevertheless, they try to incentivize them with stock options. Misguided leaders want to fit in with the dominant narrative of a strong leader, but do not grasp that they will only get the best out of their employees if they build authentic trust (dB), create a genuinely purposeful organization (dC), and make all stakeholders feel safe to interact with them (dD). Both Lawrence and Collins state that many leaders of publicly listed organizations fit this category. In recent decades, the various attempts to discover the principles of excellence in leadership and organizations have time and again confirmed that the best organizations for people to work in, to work for, to be the customer of, and invest in are those that follow the four-drive model.

Further confirming the power of the humanistic model, Google researchers found evidence from examining which of its teams were most effective. In what was called Project Aristotle, the study analyzed data from hundreds of Google teams and sought to identify patterns in team dynamics, communication styles, and individual traits that contribute to team success.[191] The study found that the most successful teams at Google shared certain key characteristics, such as psychological safety (dD), dependability and trust (dB), clear goals and accountability (dA), and purpose and meaning of work (dC). Psychological safety, in particular, emerged as a crucial factor, indicating that teams where members feel safe to take risks, express their opinions, and be vulnerable without fear of judgment or retribution tend to perform better.

Cultures that balance the four drives have been proven to outperform others that only focus on the drive to acquire.[192] Further, I highlight several organizations that have proven that humanistic management is not only possible but also very effective. Over decades, these organizations have proven that humanistic management is superior socially, environmentally, and often economically as well. I have selected globally representative businesses to demonstrate that humanistic management is possible all over the globe; as one would assume, the underlying assumptions represent human beings in a universal way.

Just to be clear, no example is perfect and leading humanistically does not mean there aren't any challenges. In fact, there are often more challenges because such organizations aim to be in service to the common good. Also, these companies are often under much more scrutiny because they represent a threat to the status quo, and a lot of criticism is motivated by a wish to delegitimize alternative management styles.

Unilever

A first example of a European company with humanistic management elements is Unilever. Unilever is a British multinational corporation specializing in consumer packaged goods. It is headquartered in London

---

[191] Google. (2024). *Google re:Work – Guides: Understand team effectiveness.* Withgoogle .com. rework.withgoogle.com/en/guides/understanding-team-effectiveness#introduction

[192] Sisodia, R., Wolfe, D., & Sheth, J. N. (2003). *Firms of endearment: How world-class companies profit from passion and purpose.* Pearson Prentice Hall.

and has a historical lineage dating back to 1929, when Lever Brothers, a British soap manufacturer, merged with the Dutch margarine producer, Margarine Unie.[193] Since then, Unilever has expanded globally, now employing approximately 127,000 individuals across 190 countries with a diverse portfolio of over 400 brands.[194] These brands are grouped into five core categories: Beauty & Wellbeing, Personal Care, Home Care, Nutrition, and Ice Cream. Despite the variety across these brand families, they are unified by a single guiding mission: to make sustainable living commonplace.[195]

Throughout its history it shifted between humanistic and economistic approaches to management. Unilever's dedication to sustainability and purpose-driven business arguably dates back to its founding. William Lever, one of the founders, established Sunlight Soap as one of the first brands with a social purpose, aimed at improving health and hygiene through accessible products.[196] Over a century later, this commitment to purposeful business practices became central once more to Unilever's operations. Under the leadership of Paul Polman, Unilever reconnected to its roots. Unilever actively leverages its global reach to promote responsible, transparent, and sustainable practices, positioning itself as a business that prioritizes long-term social impact alongside profitability.[197]

Unilever's approach under Polman, described as a "purpose-led, future-fit business model," is designed to generate both social value and business growth. According to recent data, Unilever's Sustainable Living Brands – which emphasize social and environmental responsibility – are growing 69 percent faster than the rest of the company's portfolio and contribute 75 percent of its growth.[198] Notably, seven of Unilever's ten top-performing brands, including Dove, Knorr, Persil, and Hellmann's, are part of the Sustainable Living Brand lineup, each brand addressing distinct social or environmental issues aligned with the company's broader sustainability objectives.[199]

---

[193] Jones, G. (2005). *Multinationals and global capitalism: From the nineteenth to the twenty-first century*. Oxford University Press.

[194] Unilever. (2024). *Our company*. Unilever. www.unilever.com. www.unilever.com/our-company/

[195] Ibid.

[196] Jones, G. (2005). *Multinationals and global capitalism: From the nineteenth to the twenty-first century*. Oxford University Press.

[197] Unilever. (2024). *Leading in the next era of corporate sustainability*. Unilever; Unilever PLC. www.unilever.com/sustainability/

[198] Unilever. (2019). *Unilever's purpose-led brands outperform*. Unilever. www.unilever.com/news/press-and-media/press-releases/2019/unilevers-purpose-led-brands-outperform/

[199] Ibid.

The measurable impact of Unilever's Sustainable Living Brands highlights their humanistic focus. Dove, for example, has reached over 35 million youths globally through its self-esteem initiatives, while Lifebuoy's hand-washing campaigns have educated over one billion people on hygiene practices. Vaseline's skin healing programs support vulnerable populations, and Ben & Jerry's actively campaigns for social justice and environmental sustainability. Additionally, Rin's Career Academy in India empowers rural women by providing mentorship and career resources.[200]

Former Unilever CEO Alan Jope emphasized the importance of purpose in contemporary consumer behavior, citing data that 66 percent of consumers select brands based on social stances, with over 90 percent of millennials willing to switch to purpose-driven brands.[201] Jope argued that purpose enhances brand relevance, promotes consumer engagement, and reduces price sensitivity, underscoring Unilever's ambition for all its brands to embody a clear social purpose.[202]

Internally, Unilever's humanistic management philosophy is reflected in its approach to employee welfare. In surveys, 84 percent of office employees agreed that Unilever genuinely cares about their well-being.[203] The company's Employee Assistance Program offers comprehensive support, including 24/7 counseling, stress management courses, life coaching, financial planning, and resilience training.[204] This holistic approach to employee well-being aligns with the principles of humanistic management, which prioritize respect, care, and personal growth for all employees.[205] Under pressure from economistic Wall Street observers and investors, Unilever since had to shift back to economistic approaches which led to layoffs and caused many internal quarrels and top talent to leave. This seemed to happen at some of the competition, such as Danone as well. So, while a humanistic approach is often very successful, traditional economistically

---

[200] Madzík, P. et al. (2022). Paul Polman's insights for the next generation of business… (PDF). *Journal of Global Responsibility*; Ben & Jerry's Homemade, Inc. (2023). *Ben & Jerry's Social & Environmental Assessment Report (SEAR) 2023;* Petnology. (2019, June 11). *Unilever's purpose-led, Sustainable Living Brands outperform.*

[201] Nielsen, Company. (2019). *Sustainable shoppers: Buy the change they wish to see.* Nielsen. Pirson, M. (2017). *Humanistic management: Protecting dignity and promoting well-being.* Cambridge University Press.

[202] Jope, A. (2019). *Unilever's purpose-led business model.* Speech presented at Unilever Global Conference.

[203] Unilever. (2024, April 20). *Employee health and wellbeing.* Unilever; Unilever PLC. www .unilever.com/sustainability/responsible-business/employee-wellbeing/

[204] Unilever. (2022). *Benefits, Learning & Wellbeing.* Careers.unilever.com. https://careers .unilever.com/benefits-learning-wellbeing

[205] Pirson, M. (2017). *Humanistic management: Protecting dignity and promoting well-being.* Cambridge University Press.

trained players (i.e., MBAs on Wall Street) force many publicly listed organizations back to short-term profit maximization and cost cutting.

Natura

Another example of a globally active company that has managed humanistically pretty much throughout its existence is Natura. Natura is an international cosmetics company headquartered in Brazil, stands out as the world's first and, as of 2023, the largest certified B Corporation.[206] Since its inception in 1969, Natura has grown significantly, employing over 35,000 individuals across more than 100 countries, with revenues reaching $7.9 billion in 2021.[207] The company's mission, "to nurture beauty and relationships for a better way of living and doing business," aligns with its vision of innovating to create positive economic, social, and environmental impacts.

Andrea Álvares, Natura's Chief Brand, Innovation, International, and Sustainability Officer, has articulated the company's purpose-driven philosophy. Álvares highlighted that the company aims to "become the best beauty company or group FOR the world." She emphasized the interconnectedness of their brands, which include AVON, The Body Shop, and other brands, noting: "There is a business reason why these companies were chosen, but there is also a purpose that joined us together."[208]

Natura's approach to management and sustainability reflects a deep understanding of interdependence. Álvares explained that the company recognizes its responsibility for its global impact, incorporating this awareness into a business model that measures success across financial, social, and environmental dimensions. By adopting a "triple bottom line" approach, Natura tracks indicators of value generation beyond profit, fostering a holistic evaluation of its contributions.[209] This philosophy distinguishes Natura's humanistic management practices from conventional economistic models, which often externalize social and environmental costs.

A cornerstone of Natura's humanistic ethos is its focus on well-being. It has a long-standing commitment to promoting harmonious relationships

---

[206] Aziz, A. (2022, May 11). How The World's Largest B Corp Natura (Owner of Body Shop, Avon and Aesop) Uses Purpose to Drive Performance and Well Being. *Forbes*. www.forbes.com/sites/afdhelaziz/2022/05/11/how-the-worlds-largest-b-corp-natura-owner-of-body-shop-avon-and-aesop-uses-purpose-to-drive-performance-and-wellbeing/

[207] Ibid.

[208] Ibid.

[209] Ibid.

with oneself, others, and nature through cosmetics and related rituals. These practices emphasize natural products, sustainable materials, and equitable value chains. Álvares framed this as a shift from wealth creation to well-being creation, underscoring the integration of humanistic principles into Natura's core operations.[210]

Natura's dedication to social impact extends to its treatment of employees, particularly its network of eight million consultants, most of whom are women. To measure its social impact, Natura introduced the Human Development Index (HDI) for its consultants in 2014, modeled after the United Nations Development Program's methodology. Between 2017 and 2019, the HDI of Natura consultants increased by 3.1 percent, attributed to initiatives like digital inclusion and financial education. The assessment also revealed a 1.8-percent annual HDI improvement for new consultants, reflecting the company's commitment to human dignity and well-being. This innovative use of the HDI serves as a model for measuring corporate social responsibility in the future.[211]

Trust is another pivotal element of Natura's strategy. Leaders are coached to "be genuine" and avoid opportunism or greenwashing. There are focused efforts to embed sustainability and ethical practices into the heart of business operations, such as regenerative practices, circularity, respect for human rights, fair wages, and reduced emissions. Leadership of Natura is aware that only these authentic practices build trust with consumers and society at large, contributing to long-term success.[212]

Natura exemplifies how corporations can empower people, promote dignity, and minimize environmental impact while achieving global success. By prioritizing purpose over profit and embracing humanistic management, the company has established itself as a force for positive change worldwide. Unfortunately, again, as a publicly listed company, economistically oriented forces pushed Natura to cut costs and sell off some of their global partner organizations. While Natura and others showcase the power of the humanistic management and leadership model, it always has to swim upstream against the tide of short-term, economistic actors.

---

[210] Ibid.

[211] Commitment to Life – Social. (n.d.). *Natura RI.* https://ri.naturaeco.com/en/commitment-to-life-social/

[212] Aziz, A. (2022, May 11). How The World's Largest B Corp Natura (Owner of Body Shop, Avon and Aesop) Uses Purpose to Drive Performance and WellBeing. *Forbes.* www.forbes.com/sites/afdhelaziz/2022/05/11/how-the-worlds-largest-b-corp-natura-owner-of-body-shop-avon-and-aesop-uses-purpose-to-drive-performance-and-wellbeing/

Barry-Wehmiller

In contrast to the previous example, Barry-Wehmiller is not a publicly listed company. Barry-Wehmiller is a rather unusual example of humanistic management, as it is a very traditional manufacturing firm. Barry-Wehmiller shows that humanistic management is key to enduring viability, even in markets that are seen as challenging, such as manufacturing in the American Midwest. While the majority of manufacturing companies have relocated to China or have closed, Barry-Wehmiller has found a way to stay commercially viable through "Truly Human Leadership."

Barry-Wehmiller is a global engineering and manufacturing solutions company based in St. Louis, Missouri. It was founded in 1885 and has since evolved into a diversified organization with a focus on capital equipment and engineering consulting across various industries such as packaging, paper converting, sheeting, and corrugating. Barry-Wehmiller is widely regarded as a humanistic company, primarily due to its commitment to fostering a culture of care, compassion, and ethical leadership within the workplace. This approach is encapsulated in the company's philosophy that emphasizes the importance of people and relationships in driving business success. Barry-Wehmiller's leadership, particularly under CEO Bob Chapman, has been instrumental in promoting a vision of business as a "powerful force for good," which aligns closely with humanistic principles that prioritize human dignity and flourishing.[213]

One of the core tenets of Barry-Wehmiller's humanistic approach is its focus on the well-being of employees. The company actively cultivates a culture of "companionate love," which is characterized by mutual respect, empathy, and support among team members.[214] This culture not only enhances employee morale and engagement but also contributes to improved organizational performance. Research indicates that organizations that prioritize emotional connections and supportive relationships tend to experience higher levels of employee satisfaction and productivity.[215] Barry-Wehmiller's commitment to creating a "Circle of Safety" for its

---

[213] Dam, N., & Rogers, E. (2018). People, purpose, and performance at Barry-Wehmiller: Business as a powerful force for good, 193–212. https://doi.org/10.1007/978-3-319-76306-4_14

[214] Barsade, S., & O'Neill, O. (2014). What's love got to do with it? A longitudinal study of the culture of companionate love and employee and client outcomes in a long-term care setting. *Administrative Science Quarterly, 59*(4), 551–598. https://doi.org/10.1177/0001839214538636

[215] Bartel, C., & Rockmann, K. (2024). The disease of indifference: How relational systems provide the attentional infrastructure for organizational resilience. *Strategic Organization, 22*(1), 18–48. https://doi.org/10.1177/14761270231183441

employees further exemplifies this humanistic approach, as it fosters an environment where individuals feel secure and valued.[216]

In addition to its internal culture, Barry-Wehmiller's humanistic philosophy extends to its broader impact on society. The company engages in various community-oriented initiatives and emphasizes the importance of social responsibility in its business practices.[217] By prioritizing ethical decision-making and community engagement, Barry-Wehmiller demonstrates a commitment to not only achieving financial success but also contributing positively to the communities in which it operates. This aligns with the notion that businesses have a moral obligation to act in ways that promote the well-being of society at large.[218]

In his public speeches, CEO Bob Chapman lamented the low rates of employee engagement nationally. "We have over a hundred and thirty million people in our workforce who go home every day feeling they work for a company that doesn't care about them. That is seven out of eight people in the workforce." He argued that we have the power to fix this issue today. "We just need to engage our heads and our hearts in a leadership process that validates the worth of every individual." This is in line with the focus on dignity, or intrinsic value, which humanistic management mandates. He describes an environment "where people can discover their gifts, develop their gifts, share their gifts, and – extremely important – be recognized and appreciated for doing so, which creates an opportunity for them to go home ... and have a more meaningful life of purpose." What he mentioned about developing and sharing gifts aligns with the four-drive model that underlies humanistic management theory. Speaking further on the importance of recognition, Chapman recalls an interaction with an employee. Speaking about a traditional work environment, which does not focus on recognition, the employee said that when he goes home "from that environment, you don't feel very good about yourself. And when you don't feel very good about yourself, you're not very nice to your wife." He said that

> since we've embraced this people-centric leadership, since we've embraced the idea of continuous improvement, where I have a chance to make my role better, to contribute my gifts, people ask me what I think ... Since we've done that, I go home feeling valued and better

---

[216] Ibid.

[217] Dam, N., & Rogers, E. (2018). People, purpose, and performance at Barry-Wehmiller: Business as a powerful force for good, 193–212. https://doi.org/10.1007/978-3-319-76306-4_14

[218] Ibid.

about myself. And when I go home feeling better about myself, I find I'm nicer to my wife. And believe it or not, when I'm nicer to my wife, she talks to me.

Chapman had a realization in that moment: the biggest measurable he would look for is a reduction in the divorce rate of his employees. This is interesting to explore, as many question how to measure or quantify well-being. He had recently learned from a family counselor that the most important thing in raising good kids is a good marriage. So, if children grow up seeing loving relationships, he argues, "many of the issues we face in this country will dissipate because we will have organizations that truly care about the impact they make."[219]

By focusing on value creation and "Truly Human Leadership," Barry-Wehmiller has delivered value to all of its stakeholders. That includes its almost 12,000 global team members and their families, their customers, shareholders, vendors and suppliers, and the communities in which they operate.[220] At the same time, the company has grown its financial value from USD 20 million to more than USD 3 billion. According to Bob Chapman, the company has outperformed even Warren Buffett's Berkshire Hathaway in terms of financial returns in the past decades.[221] It goes to show that human-centered management is not only beneficial for employees and communities, but it is more profitable for the company as well. As such, Barry Wehmiller's example may suggest that a humanistic model needs to be protected from the economistic actors in the public markets. It also may suggest that the short-term oriented analysts business schools prepare in their MBA programs are not a good fit for such long-term oriented organizations. Barry Wehmiller rarely hires MBAs and has opted to create its internal university to develop its people, not leaving it to traditional business schools. This should make business educators think again.

Narayana Health

To showcase the power and relevance of humanistic management and leadership, Narayana Health is an interesting example of a publicly listed healthcare organization based in India. Founded as Narayana

---

[219] TEDx Talks. (2012). Truly human leadership: Bob Chapman at TEDxScottAFB. In *YouTube*. www.youtube.com/watch?v=njn-lIEv1LU

[220] Chapman, B. (n.d.). *People, Purpose and Performance at Barry-Wehmiller: Business as a Powerful Force for Good. Executive Summary*. https://docs.ie.edu/center-for-corporate-learning-innovation/Business-as-a-Powerful-Force-for-Good.pdf

[221] www.firsthuman.com/article/profile-bob-chapman-ceo-and-champion-of-whole-human-leadership/ (accessed January 23, 2025).

Hrudayalaya Heart Hospital, Narayana Health is headquartered in Bangalore, India. Narayana Health is a leading healthcare institution renowned for its pioneering work in cardiac care. Founded by Dr. Devi Shetty in 2001, the hospital has grown to become one of the largest cardiac care facilities globally, providing highest-quality, affordable healthcare services. Narayana Health distinguishes itself not only through medical excellence but also through its commitment to humanistic principles in healthcare delivery. The hospital has adopted innovative and inclusive strategies to ensure that quality healthcare is accessible to a broad spectrum of the population.

Cardiac surgeon Dr. Devi Shetty has contained costs "by tweaking processes, driving hard bargains and negotiating creative partnership deals."[222] The hospital then passes these savings to its customers in order to fulfill their mission of affordable healthcare. Patients at Narayana Health get cardiac care at the lowest cost in the country and at a fraction of what it costs in the rest of the world, a feat accomplished through what Shetty refers to as "process innovation." Shetty was formerly personal physician to Mother Teresa, and he notes that his interactions with her "not only offered the opportunity to closely observe the famed humanitarian's charitable work but also caused the doctor to begin thinking about how quality health care could be made widely accessible and affordable."[223] To Shetty, this highlighted the need for process innovation, rather than product innovation, in the healthcare industry.

A process innovation which centers on human dignity is Narayana Health's partnerships with insurance companies. "We charge only $1,200 to $1,400 for heart operations; 80% of the country's population cannot even afford that to save their lives. How do you make it affordable to them? Eleven years ago, we launched a new microhealth-insurance scheme called Yeshasvini Microhealth Insurance," Shetty said. There are 1.7 million farmers paying 11 cents per month for the insurance, which connects 400 hospitals. The farmers can go to any of these hospitals and get any operation free of cost, besides the 11 cents per month. This radical collaboration allowed millions of people to gain access to lifesaving healthcare.

While some think it is charity, it is important to note that one of the biggest predictors of quality in healthcare is the amount of procedures a doctor has performed – a learning curve effect. With increased amounts of

---

[222] Economics, H., Asia-Pacific, & India. (2010, July 1). *Narayana Hrudayalaya: A Model for Accessible, Affordable Health Care? Knowledge@Wharton.* https://knowledge.wharton.upenn.edu/article/narayana-hrudayalaya-a-model-for-accessible-affordable-health-care/
[223] Ibid.

procedures, the quality of each procedure is increased and can therefore command higher prices from wealthier clientele. Such clientele prefers to receive the best care, and the funds received can be used to pay for the other procedures, which reinforces a virtuous cycle of increased performance.

Another innovation is that the hospital doubles as an academic institution which trains heart surgeons, cardiologists, perfusionists, and nurses. This helps the hospital cut costs. "We conduct 79 training programs on campus, so half of the workforce here is not paid by us. They are students undergoing a training program," said Shetty.[224] This not only reduces costs but also elevates the learning of the personnel and adds quality to the service.

Lastly, Narayana Health actively reaches out to underserved communities and offers charitable medical services. This commitment to social responsibility aligns with the hospital's broader mission of making a positive societal impact beyond its immediate healthcare services.

In conclusion, Narayana Health exemplifies a humanistic approach to healthcare by combining medical excellence with a commitment to affordability, accessibility, and patient-centered care. Through its innovative models, inclusive initiatives, and dedication to social responsibility, the hospital not only heals patients but also contributes to the well-being of the communities it serves. It will be interesting to observe how Narayana Health can deal with the pressures of public markets, and so far it seems to have weathered the economistic storms.

SEKEM

As a different organization entirely operating in Northern Africa, the SEKEM initiative is a humanistic conglomerate built to serve Egypt and the well-being of its people. SEKEM was founded in 1977 by Dr. Ibrahim Abouleish and has become a renowned sustainable development initiative. The SEKEM initiative was founded with the mission to promote sustainable human development. It began as a small-scale agricultural project and has since evolved to encompass several businesses in agriculture, education, healthcare, as well as cultural initiatives. SEKEM, which means *vitality from the sun,* is widely recognized for its commitment to holistic human development, combining economic success with social responsibility and environmental stewardship. The company's humanistic principles

---

[224] Tam, E., & Messmer, L. (2015, September 16). Heart Surgeon Brings High-Tech Health Care to the World's Poor. WSJ; *The Wall Street Journal.* www.wsj.com/articles/heart-surgeon-brings-high-tech-healthcare-to-the-worlds-poor-1442391424

are deeply rooted in its founder's vision of fostering human dignity, community building, and sustainable practices.

In 1997, troubled by the social problems and poverty he saw while visiting his home country, Dr. Abouleish moved his family to Egypt from their comfortable life in Austria. In 2003, he was the first entrepreneur to receive the "Right Livelihood Award," also widely known as the "Alternative Nobel Prize." From the 2003 press release:

> SEKEM (Egypt) shows how a modern business can combine profitability and engagement in world markets with a humane and spiritual approach to people and respect for the natural environment. The Jury sees in SEKEM "a business model for the 21st century in which commercial success is integrated with and promotes the social and cultural development of society through the economics of love."[225]

Abouleish bought some untouched desert land hoping to reclaim the land to produce natural medicines and food. Despite initial pushback, Abouleish's team constructed wells and planted 120,000 trees to provide shade and shelter for plants and animals. The team promoted soil fertility through the use of organic compost, which was produced on-site from animal waste. They built electricity and water systems, roads, and houses. All of these measures would eventually help SEKEM to become profitable, but the primary intention and result was to create value out of land that had been considered worthless. The regeneration of the environment and the construction of infrastructure generated both environmental and social benefit.

SEKEM initially faced a series of setbacks from the Egyptian army and government. Abouleish had to defend himself to the government on multiple fronts, but was eventually allowed to continue with supervision from the administration. This collaboration actually proved beneficial to SEKEM in the long term, as it increased the company's credibility and allowed it to expand its reach through government partnership. For example, SEKEM's development of biodynamic cultivation methods for cotton in 1992 was revolutionary for the entire country. The trial results convinced the government to stop dispensing 35,000 tons of pesticides per year, which previously were sprayed from the air to the detriment of the health of farmers and communities. Not only has the innovation improved living conditions, but the cotton yields were higher and the cotton was of

---

[225] Mair, J., & Seelos, C. (2024). *Harvard Business Publishing Education*. Harvard.edu. https://hbsp.harvard.edu/download?url=%2Fcourses%2F1210613%2Fitems%2F IES129-PDF-ENG%2Fcontent&metadata=e30%3D

better quality. Approximately 850 farms are now members of the Egyptian Biodynamic Association, which advises and instructs farmers and promotes biodynamic agriculture in Egypt on a scientific basis. This commitment to sharing knowledge aligns with and promotes the human drive to comprehend.

Today, SEKEM is a group of nine successful companies that export organic food, spices, tea, medicine, and cotton. All farms use the biodynamic method, which employs natural processes and refrains from chemical usage. The pharmaceutical division of SEKEM also applies high standards to its materials, helping the body to activate its natural functions without side effects. The clothing division applies environmentally friendly treatments to its organically grown cotton to produce fine and breathable garments. SEKEM employees start their work day by meeting in a circle, which represents equality and the unity of their shared vision. SEKEM believes that "like any living organism, the vital network of the SEKEM community needs well-functioning organs – social institutions which secure rights and claim responsibility – organizations which set rules to guarantee equality and social and judicial structures in which the individual is able to recognize his own dignity and therefore is encouraged to help himself."[226] The co-operative of SEKEM employees, described as an independent judicial organ, is central to the organization's social structure. The cooperative informs team members about their rights and responsibilities, promotes living standards, establishes social funds, coordinates training programs, and promotes cooperation between SEKEM and the government. These efforts demonstrate SEKEM's commitment to the comprehensive development of the individual, society, and environment.[227] SEKEM is not publicly listed and integrates many different services and products under its name. Yet, the overarching philosophy is humanistically oriented, and while small, it keeps inspiring leaders globally about what is possible.

Conclusion

The reality proves feasibility. The businesses and leaders previously mentioned represent a globally representative but small sliver of what exists and what is possible. Many more examples of humanistic businesses exist,

---

[226] Faisal Mirza. (2010, June 16). *SEKEM English Part 1*. YouTube. www.youtube.com/watch?v=BXXpamUjYmg

[227] Mair, J., & Seelos, C. (2024). *Harvard Business Publishing Education*. Harvard.edu. https://hbsp.harvard.edu/download?url=%2Fcourses%2F1210613%2Fitems%2FIES129-PDF-ENG%2Fcontent&metadata=e30%3D

including Mondragon, Gore, Patagonia, or DM, just to name a few. These organizations prove that humanity can do better, as many of us want to do better. Many argue that a change in consciousness is needed to change the quality of leadership, the quality of organizations, and the quality of our society. Others suggest that we need to increase our awareness of what it means to be human. The humanistic model of human nature is an opportunity for management researchers and practitioners to increase such awareness and share the power of what is possible when our business practices become more human.

7 Humanistic Leadership

> Normal is getting dressed in clothes that you buy for work and driving through traffic in a car that you are still paying for in order to get to a job that you need to pay for the clothes and the car and the house you leave vacant all day so that you can afford to live in it.[228]

The term leadership seems more fashionable than management. And many collaborators in the field such as Bob Chapman prefer to use the term leadership over management. They view management as manipulation. In our understanding, of course, the protection of dignity – that is, the absence of exploitation – is critical. And yet, if we use the lens of leadership, we can imagine a humanistic form of leadership and develop an approach that focuses on the *person* and the *process*.

Humanistic Leadership: Of Sandwiches and Bagels

In my teaching, I describe our current mindsets as best represented by a triangular American-style Bologna sandwich, standing on its side, sloping upward. It represents the dominant idea that all we want is MORE – growth, unlimited growth, and good leadership provides that (Figure 4).

Kate Raworth, however, has proposed that we change the imagery of our economic system to resemble a donut.[229] The core of the donut – the "munchkin" – represents what I call the dignity core, the basic needs of all humans to live as humans. The outer boundary of the donut represents the planetary boundaries that humanity is violating – at our peril (Figure 5).

When I bring donuts for my students, inevitably half of them do not want to eat them because they are unhealthy. So much so that Dunkin'

---

[228] https://quodid.com/quotes/1272/ellen-goodman/normal-is-getting-dressed-in-clothes-that-you (accessed January 24, 2025).

[229] Raworth, K. (2017). *Doughnut economics: Seven ways to think like a 21st-century economist*. Chelsea Green Publishing.

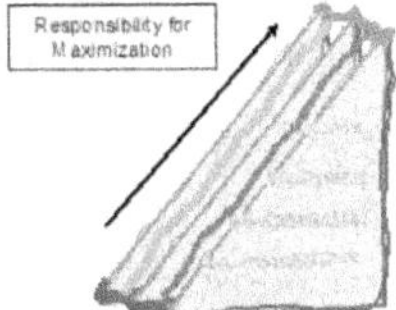

Figure 4 Economistic model: Responsibility for maximization (own graphic)

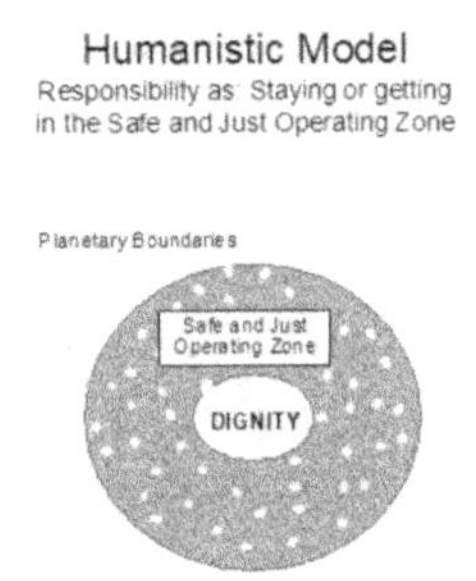

Figure 5 Humanistic model (own depiction based on Raworth (2017))

Donuts, one of the largest chains in the United States, decided to drop the name "Donuts" because millennials and others do not like it. I have since resorted to bringing along more wholesome bagels.

I agree with Kate Raworth that metaphors shape the way we think, see, and act in the world. I am suggesting that bagel management is a better idea for how we should understand the task of managers and leaders.

Using the bagel as a metaphor better suited to my students, I now argue that the most important task of managers is to:

- move humanity above the dignity threshold (the inner core), and
- reduce the impact of human activity on the planetary boundaries, to
- enable flourishing of all life on earth.

Kate Raworth suggests we call the zone we need to be moving to the "safe and just operating zone for humanity."[230] I call the process we need to get there "humanistic leadership": the protection of dignity and the promotion of well-being.

---

[230] Ibid.

Creating a New Normal

As the Ellen Goodman quote at the start of this section indicates, our current understanding of normal is bizarre. There are plenty of ways to live a better and more fulfilling life. Yet, in our educational efforts we seem to endorse the hustle and bustle approach to creating wealth as a signifier of human value. Our societal leaders at large personify such economistic values. Therefore, if we want more people to embrace more fulfilling lives and address the issues of our times, we need to go deeper and address personal development and formation.

To develop ourselves and support others in the development of humanistic leaders, a group of scholars has created the Humanistic Leadership Academy.[231] In that context, we aim to present an integral approach to personal development around knowing, doing, and being a humanistic leader.[232] In this way, we uncover some of the intellectual foundations on which the current system is built and create alternative options. Such alternatives allow for choice, and mostly when they have a choice people opt for the more life-conducive option. After all, we are a product of nature and nature regenerates life.

The baseline for the humanistic personal development process is a new realism about who we are as people. Many of us have unknowingly bought into one or another form of veneer theory – the idea that we are fundamentally bad, asocial, amoral, and seek to disguise that to allow for egotistic social purposes.[233]

Critics of veneer theory, like primatologist Frans de Waal, argue that morality is more deeply rooted in our evolutionary history, arising from the social nature of primates, including humans.[234] De Waal and others propose that traits such as empathy, cooperation, and fairness evolved as beneficial adaptations that helped early human societies survive and thrive.[235] Charles Darwin's views on morality, particularly in *The Descent of Man*, suggest that morality evolved as part of human nature, shaped by social instincts that promote cooperation and empathy. Darwin argued that the roots of morality lie in the social behaviors seen in other animals,

---

[231] For more information: www.humanisticleadershipacademy.org

[232] Pirson, M. et al. (2025). Humanistic Leadership Academy – a Multi Stakeholder Effort towards Educating for Human Flourishing, The Elgar Companion to Management Education and the UN Sustainable Development Goals, editors Wall, Girei, Antonacopoulou, Blasco, Nkomo& Ogunyemi in Edward Elgar Publishers.

[233] Bregman, R. (2020). *Humankind: A hopeful history*. Bloomsbury Publishing.

[234] De Waal, F. B. (2014). Natural normativity: The 'is' and 'ought' of animal behavior. *Behaviour, 151*(2–3), 185–204.

[235] De Waal, F. (2010). *The age of empathy: Nature's lessons for a kinder society*. Crown.

particularly in primates, which exhibit compassion, care for the young, and cooperation within groups.[236] Much current research confirms that rather than being a mere cover, morality is seen as an integral part of human nature, shaped by both biology and culture.[237] As Rutger Bregman writes in his book *Humankind,* most people are decent, and if our perspectives on human nature shift, it will create many new possibilities for collaboration.[238] As we embrace this "new normal," we can lead our own lives and interact with others, opening up new possibilities.

A big challenge to humanistic leadership is that it requires consistent personal development. Bob Kegan's Constructive Developmental Theory and Ken Wilber's Integral Theory provide valuable frameworks for understanding humanistic management and personal development.[239,240] Both theories emphasize the importance of ongoing development throughout adulthood, integrating cognitive, emotional, and social dimensions of human experience.

Not Everyone Is Equal

While it is fashionable to posit equality, it is important to note that there are hierarchies in personal development. Some people are more willing to engage in it and develop along so-called growth hierarchies. Such growth hierarchies are distinct from more traditional dominator hierarchies.

Growth hierarchies refer to systems where hierarchy exists to support development, empowerment, and growth for all individuals involved. These hierarchies are not about power or control, but about nurturing potential and ensuring the well-being of the collective. The primary goal is to facilitate learning, collaboration, and mutual upliftment. Leaders, or those higher up in the hierarchy, use their positions to guide and help others grow, providing opportunities for development.

Unfortunately, most business education is about developing dominator hierarchies in which the focus is the gaining and maintaining of power, often at the expense of others. As a result, in many well-intentioned conversations the conflation of growth and domination-oriented hierarchies

---

[236] Darwin, C., & Griffith, T. (1874). *The descent of man* (Vol. 4). Prometheus Books.

[237] Greene, J. (2014). *Moral tribes: Emotion, reason, and the gap between us and them.* Penguin.

[238] Bregman, R. (2020). *Humankind: A hopeful history.* Bloomsbury Publishing.

[239] Kegan, R. (1982). *The evolving self: Problem and process in human development.* Harvard University Press.

[240] Wilber, K. (2000). *Integral psychology: Consciousness, spirit, psychology, therapy.* Shambhala Publications.

leaves humanistic leadership powerless. The solution to this is seen as trying to avoid dominator hierarchies, focusing on "everyone is equal," and abolishing hierarchies. This is important to note, as it has massive implications for business education and corporate development. In a humanistic context, the only journey to leadership is the "journey within."

Conclusion

When we start to embrace the "new normal" according to humanistic principles and understand that we are responsible for our own "inner journey," we automatically honor our own dignity. Then, and only then, will we start to flourish. Once we are in this mindset, we can develop ourselves as humanistic leaders, embracing others and collaborating authentically to create a world that works for all of us. Humanistic leaders are on a journey. On that journey, they typically find that many people around them yearn to make an authentic contribution to the common good. But many of them do not yet have the skills, knowledge, or experience to see how. That is the big opportunity for humanistic leaders to step in and up. I invite you all to continue this journey.

To my mother Renate and my father Wolfgang Pirson

Cambridge Elements ᵇ

Business Strategy

J.-C. Spender
Rutgers Business School

J.-C. Spender is a visiting scholar at Rutgers Business School and a research Professor, Kozminski University. He has been active in the business strategy field since 1971 and is the author or co-author of 7 books and numerous papers. His principal academic interest is in knowledge-based theories of the private sector firm, and managing them.

Advisory Board

Jay Barney, *Eccles School of Business, The University of Utah*
Stewart Clegg, *University of Technology, Sydney*
Thomas Durand, *Conservatoire National des Arts et Métiers, Paris*
CT Foo, *Independent Scholar, Singapore*
Robert Grant, *Bocconi University, Milan*
Robin Holt, *Copenhagen Business School*
Paula Jarzabkowski, *Cass School, City University, London*
Naga Lakshmi Damaraju, *Indian School of Business*
Marjorie Lyles, *Kelley School of Business, Indiana University*
Joseph T. Mahoney, *College of Business, University of Illinois at Urbana Champaign*
Nicolai Foss, *Bocconi University, Milan*
Andreas Scherer, *University of Zurich*
Deepak Somaya, *College of Business, University of Illinois at Urbana-Champaign*
Eduard van Gelderen, *Chief Investment Officer, APG, Amsterdam*

About the Series

Business strategy's reach is vast, and important too since wherever there is business activity there is strategizing. As a field, strategy has a long history from medieval and colonial times to today's developed and developing economies. This series offers a place for interesting and illuminating research including industry and corporate studies, strategizing in service industries, the arts, the public sector, and the new forms of Internet-based commerce. It also covers today's expanding gamut of analytic techniques.

Cambridge Elements ≡

Business Strategy

Elements in the Series

Strategizing in the Polish Furniture Industry
Paulina Bednarz-Łuczewska

A Historical Review of Swedish Strategy Research and the Rigor-Relevance Gap
Thomas Kalling and Lars Bengtsson

Global Strategy in Our Age of Chaos: How Will the Multinational Firm Survive?
Stephen Tallman and Mitchell P. Koza

Strategizing with Institutional Theory
Harry Sminia

Effectuation: Rethinking Fundamental Concepts in the Social Sciences
Saras Sarasvathy

Behavioral Strategy: Exploring Microfoundations of Competitive Advantage
Nicolai J. Foss, Ambra Mazzelli and Libby Weber

Digital Assets: A Portfolio Perspective
Henrique Schneider

Diversification in the World of Data and AI
Gianvito Lanzolla and Constantinos Markides

Dynamic Capabilities and Related Paradigms
David J. Teece

Dynamic Capabilities: Foundational Concepts
David J. Teece

The Demise of the Global ICE Industry: China's Stunning Role in Leading the BEV Revolution
Arie Lewin, Martin Kenney, EI (Emily) Shu and Liang Mei

Humanistic Management and Leadership
Michael Pirson

A full series listing is available at: www.cambridge.org/EBUS

For EU product safety concerns, contact us at Calle de José Abascal, 56–1°,
28003 Madrid, Spain or eugpsr@cambridge.org.

www.ingramcontent.com/pod-product-compliance
Lightning Source LLC
LaVergne TN
LVHW020109220526
839337LV00035B/429

9 781009 698443